Amandeep Bains is a solicitor at Duncan Lewis Solicitors specialising in housing law and property litigation. He has extensive experience acting for individuals and families in homelessness applications, statutory reviews, county court appeals, judicial review proceedings and higher court litigation, with a particular focus on challenging decision-making by local housing authorities. He holds an LLB (Hons), an LLM with a specialism in homelessness law, and the LPC, and is recognised for his commitment to access to justice and is included on the pro bono list for England and Wales (2026).

A Practical Guide to Homelessness Law in England

A Practical Guide to Homelessness Law in England

Amandeep Bains LLB (Hons), LLM and LPC
Solicitor, Duncan Lewis Solicitors

Law Brief Publishing

Published 2026 by Law Brief Publishing, an imprint of Law Brief Publishing Ltd
30 The Parks
Minehead
Somerset
TA24 8BT

www.lawbriefpublishing.com

Paperback: 978-1-918241-35-8

PREFACE

This guide traces the course of a homelessness application, following it from first contact through to the legal remedy. It reflects both the statutory framework and the real-world experiences of those who work within it: lawyers, advisers, and decision-makers alike.

Part 1: Foundations of Homelessness Law introduces the purpose, and structure of the statutory scheme. It considers how the Housing Act 1996 and the Homelessness Reduction Act 2017 impose enforceable duties on local authorities, and it highlights how those duties are structured, triggered, and brought to an end. It also examines the role of human rights, equality obligations, and the courts in shaping and supervising homelessness decision-making, providing the legal context within which all subsequent statutory tests and procedural duties operate.

Part 2: Core Statutory Tests addresses the principal legal questions that decide entitlement to assistance: eligibility, homelessness, priority need, intentionality and local connection. Each chapter draws together legislation, statutory guidance and case law to show how these tests are applied in practice.

Part 3: Procedure, Decision-Making and Remedies outlines how the homelessness scheme is operated in practice. It follows the route from first approach, through the inquiries and assessments a local authority ought to make, to the decisions it must give and the duties it must then perform or lawfully end. It also sets out the routes by which those decisions are corrected or challenged, whether by review, appeal, or judicial review, and it identifies the practical standards that the law requires of those administering the scheme.

This book is designed to be used flexibly. Decision makers may consult it during active casework; advisers may turn to it for a structured overview of housing law; and may rely on it to understand applicants' rights and the process they face.

Ultimately, the aim is to make homelessness law clear and usable. The law should operate as a means of justice, not a barrier to it.

Disclaimer – Practical Guidance Only

This book provides general information and procedural guidance on homelessness law and practice in England. It is intended as a practical reference for solicitors, barristers, housing advisers, and informed readers in seeking to understand the rights and duties of both applicants and local authorities.

It is not a substitute for independent legal advice. Homelessness law is complex, fact-sensitive and constantly evolving through legislation, statutory guidance and case law. Every case depends on its particular circumstances, and the law may have changed after publication.

Anyone who is homeless or threatened with homelessness, or anyone acting on behalf of such a person, should seek specific advice from a qualified solicitor, barrister or accredited housing adviser before taking any action.

Case law and statutory materials are referred to selectively to illustrate key principles and practical application. References are not intended to be exhaustive, and the omission of any authority should not be taken to indicate that it is not relevant or applicable.

Neither the author nor the publisher accepts responsibility for loss or damage arising from reliance on the material in this book without proper professional advice.

All statutory references and case law are correct as of 2nd February 2026, unless otherwise stated.

About This Book – Purpose and Use

A Practical Guide to Homelessness Law in England is intended to explain, in plain and practical terms, how the law on homelessness works in everyday situations.

It aims to close the gap between detailed legal analysis and the realities of day-to-day decision-making. The book is written for applicant's advisors, local authorities and lawyers, offering a clear route through the statutory framework.

Each chapter mirrors the typical path of a homelessness case under Part VII of the Housing Act 1996, as amended by the Homelessness Reduction Act 2017. It addresses:

- The legal duties owed by local authorities;
- The key statutory tests (eligibility, homelessness, priority need, intentionality and local connection); and
- The procedure, review, appeal and judicial remedies available when things go wrong.

Drawing on front-line experience of housing and homelessness law, this guide aims to translate complex legislation into practical guidance that lawyers, local authorities and advisors can apply directly to the cases before them.

Amandeep Bains
April 2026

ACKNOWLEDGEMENTS

This book is dedicated to all those working to protect housing rights.

It grew out of my daily work representing people at some of the most difficult and defining moments of their lives. Homelessness law deals with real and often urgent circumstances, shaping decisions that affect families and people seeking safety and individuals trying to secure a roof over their heads.

Every client, every hearing and every conversation has shown me how much is at stake for the people behind each case.

My sincere gratitude goes to Mrs Manjinder Kaur Atwal, Director at Duncan Lewis Solicitors, who has been a constant source of encouragement and support throughout my career. Your judgment, the standards you set and the way you lead by example have taught me more than I can properly set out here.

To Mr Daljit Singh Shina, Director at Duncan Lewis Solicitors, thank you for your mentorship, patience and willingness to share your knowledge have been invaluable. Your guidance has shaped my professional development and this book alike.

To Mr Toby Vanhegan, Barrister at 4–5 Gray's Inn Square, it has been a privilege to work with you on so many cases and to learn from your exceptional knowledge, especially in homelessness law and housing law. Your insight and clarity of thought have had a lasting impact on my understanding of this area and on my approach as a lawyer.

And finally, my sincere thanks to Mr Ginda Basra, Lead of Team Leicester at the Midland Langar Seva Society, and to everyone involved in the charity's work, for the opportunity to work alongside you. Your commitment to supporting people experiencing homelessness at the frontline, offering not only food but practical assistance, demonstrated what genuine public service requires. The experience I gained with MLSS formed an important part of my early understanding of homelessness work and continues to inform my approach and judgment today.

CONTENTS

PART ONE

FOUNDATIONS OF HOMELESSNESS LAW

As set out in the introduction to this book, homelessness law in England is a central part of the statutory housing regime. It regulates the duties imposed upon local authorities where an individual or household is homeless or threatened with homelessness. The framework is public, procedural, and administrative in character. It prescribes how local authorities must determine eligibility, undertake inquiries, and discharge housing functions in accordance with the Housing Act 1996.

Homelessness law defines the extent of public responsibility and the limitations of discretion. It establishes the statutory structure within which local authorities operate and the mechanisms through which their decisions are reviewed or challenged. The legislation functions both as a regulatory framework for service delivery and as a legal control on the exercise of public power.

The system draws upon primary and secondary legislation, statutory guidance, and judicial interpretation, each of which plays a distinct role in shaping how homelessness decisions are made and challenged. An understanding of its structure, and procedural sequence is essential for lawyers, applicant's advisors and decision-makers working within it.

CHAPTER ONE

THE PURPOSE AND FRAMEWORK OF HOMELESSNESS LAW

1.1 Statutory Framework

Part VII of the Housing Act 1996, as amended by subsequent legislation including the Homelessness Reduction Act 2017, provides the principal statutory framework governing homelessness in England. The Homelessness Code of Guidance for Local Authorities, in conjunction with section 182 of the 1996 Act, sets out the Government's view on the proper interpretation and application of these provisions and should be taken into account by local authorities when exercising their homelessness functions.

The duties under Part VII are deliberately structured in sequence. Each stage is governed by defined legal thresholds, procedural requirements, and time limits. The scheme is designed to promote early intervention, structured assessment, and graduated responses to housing loss, while ensuring that decision-making remains legally accountable at every stage.

- **Initial duty to make inquiries**

  If a local authority has reason to believe that an applicant may be homeless or threatened with homelessness, it must make such inquiries as are necessary to determine what duty, if any, is owed under section 184. The threshold is intentionally low and does not require proof, per se. While inquiries are ongoing, the local authority may be required to secure interim accommodation under section 188 if there is reason to believe that the applicant may be homeless, eligible for assistance, and in priority need.

- **Assessment duty**

  Under section 189A, the local authority must assess the applicant's circumstances, housing needs, and the support required to secure accommodation. That assessment ordinarily results in a Personalised Housing Plan, setting out the reasonable steps to be taken by both the local authority and the applicant. Likewise, this assessment underpins the prevention and relief stages and is a mandatory procedural step and is not a discretionary exercise, where applicable.

- **Prevention duty**

  Section 195 imposes a duty on the local authority to take reasonable steps to prevent homelessness where it is satisfied that the applicant is threatened with homelessness within 56 days. The duty is forward-looking and continues until it is brought to an end in one of the ways prescribed by statute.

- **Relief duty**

  Section 189B requires the local authority to take reasonable steps to help a homeless applicant secure suitable accommodation that is available for occupation for at least six months. The duty ordinarily lasts for a maximum of 56 days unless lawfully ended earlier. Subject to eligibility, it applies regardless of priority need.

- **Main housing duty**

  Section 193 imposes the main housing duty where the applicant remains homeless after the relief stage and is eligible for assistance, in priority need, and not intentionally homeless. This duty requires the local authority to secure suitable accommodation until it is lawfully discharged and represents the highest level of statutory protection within the scheme.

- **Suitability**

  Section 206 provides that any accommodation secured under Part VII must be suitable. Suitability is not confined to physical condition. It requires consideration of affordability, location, accessibility, and the applicant's household circumstances. It is a question of mixed fact and law and ought to be assessed on an individual basis. Suitability remains open to review and challenge for as long as the duty continues.

- **Termination and notification**

  Statutory duties may be brought to an end through acceptance of suitable accommodation, refusal of a suitable offer, deliberate and unreasonable refusal to co-operate, or other prescribed statutory grounds. Any decision to end a duty must be notified to the applicant in writing, it ought to explain the reasons for the decision, and must set out the applicant's rights to request a review and, where applicable, to appeal.

- **Review and appeal**

  Applicants have a statutory right to request a review of most homelessness decisions under section 202, followed by a right of appeal to the County Court on a point of law under section 204. These mechanisms provide structured internal and external oversight and are central to the integrity of the statutory scheme.

Throughout the process, local authorities are required to maintain accurate and updated records of inquiries, assessments, and decisions. Although the Code of Guidance does not have the force of statute, departures from it should be justified by clear and lawful reasons. Part VII works as a single scheme in which procedural discipline and substantive duties reinforce each other to ensure that homelessness functions are exercised lawfully, transparently, and in accordance with public law principles.

1.2 Decision-Making Structure

Decision-making under Part VII follows a prescribed sequence. When an eligible person approaches a local authority for assistance, the first question is whether the local authority has reason to believe that the applicant may be homeless or threatened with homelessness. If that threshold is met, the local authority must make inquiries under section 184, and the interim accommodation duty under section 188 may arise if there is reason to believe the applicant may be homeless, eligible, and in priority need.

The local authority ought then to determine the following statutory questions:

- Is the applicant eligible for assistance, having regard to immigration status and any applicable residence requirements?
- Is the applicant homeless, or threatened with homelessness within 56 days?
- Does the applicant have a priority need?
- Is the applicant homeless intentionally?
- Does the applicant have a local connection with the area, or should the case be referred to another local authority?

Each question requires a separate and evidence-based assessment. The local authority should obtain relevant information, make appropriate enquiries, and verify material where necessary. In practice, this will often involve interviews, contact with landlords or other agencies, examination of notices and tenancy documentation, and consideration of medical or support evidence where relevant. The decision-maker must avoid treating the statutory tests as a single blended judgment: a conclusion on priority need, for example, cannot substitute for proper reasoning on eligibility, and a finding of homelessness does not answer the separate question of intentionality.

The outcome of the inquiries must be recorded and notified in writing under section 184. The notification should identify the decision reached on the relevant statutory questions, specify what duty (if any) is owed, and explain the applicant's right to request a review under section 202. In the event the local authority relies on disputed facts, the decision letter should make clear what findings have been made, the evidential basis for those findings, and why contrary material has been rejected.

In this regard, it should be noted that a failure to make adequate inquiries, to give proper reasons, or to reach decisions within a reasonable period may render decision-making unlawful and open to challenge through the statutory review and appeal framework, and in appropriate cases by public law proceedings.

1.3 Human Rights and the Human Dimension

Local authorities exercising functions under Part VII of the Housing Act 1996 are required to act in accordance with the Human Rights Act 1998 and the Equality Act 2010. These statutes do not create free-standing homelessness duties, but they shape how statutory powers and discretions should be exercised and how decisions are reached.

Article 8 of the European Convention on Human Rights, incorporated into domestic law by the Human Rights Act 1998, protects the right to respect for private and family life and the home. Whilst Article 8 does not confer a general right to housing, homelessness decisions may have to take into account Article 8 interests where they affect an individual's existing home, family relationships, or settled way of life. In such cases, a local authority should ensure that its decisions are lawful, and proportionate to the legitimate aim pursued. A failure to consider the impact of a decision on family life, particularly where children or vulnerable adults are involved, may render the decision unlawful.

The Equality Act 2010 imposes the Public Sector Equality Duty under section 149 (PSED). When exercising homelessness functions, a local authority ought to have due regard to the need to:

- eliminate unlawful discrimination, harassment, and victimisation;
- advance equality of opportunity between persons who share a protected characteristic and those who do not; and
- foster good relations between different groups.

The duty is procedural and substantive. It requires conscious and timely consideration of equality implications as part of the decision-making process, and not a retrospective justification after the event. Compliance should therefore be demonstrated through the reasoning process and the decision record. A failure to identify relevant protected characteristics, or to consider how a decision may disproportionately affect a particular group, is likely to amount to a breach of section 149 and may invalidate the decision.

Human rights and equality obligations regulate the manner in which homelessness functions are carried out. They do not alter the substantive tests under Part VII per se, nor do they displace the statutory criteria for eligibility, priority need, intentionality, local connection or suitability. Their function is to ensure that statutory powers are exercised lawfully, rationally, and with proper regard to the rights and interests involved in each individual case.

1.4 Role of the Courts

The courts ensure that local authorities act within the limits of their statutory powers and comply with the legal standards that govern public decision-making. In homelessness law, this supervision is not concerned with substituting the court's view for that of the local authority on the merits. Its function is to ensure that statutory tests are applied correctly, that inquiries are adequate, that reasons are intelligible, and that decisions are reached lawfully and fairly.

There are three primary mechanisms for challenge:

- **Internal review**

  Section 202 of the Housing Act 1996 provides for review of specified homelessness decisions by a reviewing officer who was not involved in the original decision. The review is the primary statutory mechanism for correcting factual and legal errors within the local authority's decision-making process.

- **Statutory appeal**

  Section 204 provides for an appeal to the County Court on a point of law. The usual route is an appeal under section 204(1)(a) against the decision on review. Section 204(1)(b) provides a separate route where the local authority has failed to notify the applicant of the review decision within the period by which notification should have been given. In addition, section 204A provides a right of appeal to the County Court against a local authority's refusal to exercise its discretion to accommodate pending a section 204 appeal under section 204(4).

- **Judicial review**

  The High Court's jurisdiction may be invoked where a local authority acts unlawfully, commits procedural error, or delays unreasonably, and where the statutory review and appeal mechanisms are not available or are not capable of providing an effective remedy in time. Judicial review does not re-try the case; instead it scrutinises legality, rationality, and procedural fairness.

Judicial interpretation of key statutory terms has shaped the practical operation of Part VII. It clarifies concepts such as "homelessness," "vulnerability," "suitability," "intentional homelessness," and the proper approach to statutory inquiries and reasons. This body of case law ensures consistency of interpretation across local authorities and maintains adherence to the statutory purpose.

Local authorities are required to apply the law as interpreted by the courts. A failure to do so may result in decisions being quashed, matters being remitted for re-determination, or mandatory orders or declarations being made where appropriate.

CHAPTER TWO

THE LEGAL DUTIES IN DETAIL

Homelessness law in England operates through a structured sequence of statutory duties. They determine, in direct and practical terms, whether a person facing the loss of their home will receive assistance, and if so, of what kind. Each duty marks a distinct stage in a local authority's exercise of its functions in respect of an applicant, beginning with prevention, progressing through relief, and, where the statutory criteria are met, culminating in the main housing duty

Although these duties operate in sequence and are closely connected, what happens at one stage can directly lead to what follows. Failures to respond properly at an early point often can have serious and lasting consequences further down the line. For that reason, it is essential for advisers and decision-makers to understand how each duty arises, what it requires, and the ways in which it can lawfully be brought to an end.

The Homelessness Reduction Act 2017 significantly altered this landscape by introducing the prevention and relief duties. Its purpose was to shift focus towards early intervention and shared responsibility between the applicant and the local authority. The traditional main housing duty under section 193 of the Housing Act 1996, however, remains in place as the final safety net for those whose homelessness cannot be resolved earlier in the process.

2.1 The Prevention Duty (s.195)

The prevention duty is the statutory mechanism for early intervention. It arises where a local authority is satisfied that an applicant is (a) threatened with homelessness within 56 days and (b) eligible for assistance.

The duty is therefore triggered by a legal assessment, and it applies to any eligible applicant who falls within the statutory definition of threatened with homelessness.

The purpose of the duty is practical and defined: the local authority must take reasonable steps to help the applicant to secure that accommodation does not cease to be available for their occupation, and—where that is not achievable—to help the applicant secure alternative accommodation before actual homelessness occurs.

At this stage, the local authority is not required to determine priority need or intentional homelessness as conditions of assistance; those questions may become material later in the statutory sequence. The prevention duty is, accordingly, intended to operate across a broad cohort of eligible applicants, with the content of "reasonable steps" determined by the facts of the individual case.

<u>What does this look like in practice?</u>

Once the duty is accepted, the local authority must carry out an assessment under section 189A and produce a Personalised Housing Plan (PHP) that records the reasonable steps to be taken by both the local authority and the applicant.

The assessment should address the circumstances giving rise to the threatened homelessness, the applicant's housing needs, the resources available to them, and any constraints that bear on the realistic options, including household composition, income, health or support needs, and risks such as domestic abuse where relevant. The PHP then functions as the working document against which progress is monitored and reviewed, and it is also likely to be central evidence if later questions arise about co-operation, suitability, or the adequacy of the steps taken.

Reasonable steps will vary, but they should be adequate, reasonable and evidenced. Depending on the cause of the threatened homelessness, they may include negotiating with a landlord to withdraw or defer housing possession action, assisting with welfare benefit issues, arranging Discretionary Housing Payments to address a short-term affordability gap, facilitating access to debt advice, or helping the applicant to identify and secure alternative accommodation. The critical point is that steps should be reasonable, recorded, and kept under review; a prevention duty cannot lawfully be reduced to signposting or generic advice where active steps are reasonably available.

It also ought to be noted that the prevention duty does not "expire" after 56 days. It continues until it is brought to an end in one of the statutory ways. As the Code of Guidance explains, the duty ends where the applicant becomes actually homeless (at which point the relief duty is triggered), and it may also be ended by notice in a defined set of circumstances, which include the securing of suitable accommodation available for at least six months and, in appropriate cases, a deliberate and unreasonable refusal to co-operate with a step in the PHP following the statutory warning and notice procedure.

As the legislation prescribes formal routes for ending the duty, a local authority should treat "ending" decisions as decisions requiring clear records, a lawful evidential basis, and a clear notification in writing.

Finally, although successful prevention will often depend on timing, the legal focus throughout remains whether the local authority has taken reasonable steps on the evidence and whether it has complied with the assessment and planning duties at the prevention stage. Without those elements in place, the prevention duty risks becoming procedural in name only, which is precisely what the 2017 reforms were intended to avoid.

2.2 The Relief Duty (s.189B)

When the prevention duty has not succeeded, or where the applicant is already homeless at the point of approach for homeless assistance, the local authority should move to the relief duty. The relief duty comes into effect under section 189B once the local authority is satisfied that the applicant is homeless and eligible for assistance.

The purpose of the relief duty is defined by statute. The local authority must take reasonable steps to help the applicant secure suitable accommodation that is available for occupation for at least six months. As with the prevention duty, the content of "reasonable steps" depends on the facts of the individual case and must be informed by the housing needs assessment and Personalised Housing Plan prepared under section 189A.

Reasonable steps during the relief stage may include:

- identifying and securing suitable private rented accommodation, including assistance with deposits or rent guarantees where appropriate;

- engaging with registered providers or supported housing schemes;

- negotiating with landlords to overcome barriers to access, such as affordability or referencing concerns; or

- coordinating with support services where accommodation is linked to care or supervision needs.

In practice, the emphasis on the relief duty remains on practical, evidence-based action rather than generic advice. Steps taken should be recorded, reviewed, and adjusted where an applicant's circumstances change.

During the relief stage, the interim accommodation duty under section 188 may continue to play a critical role. Once the local authority has reason to believe that the applicant may be homeless, eligible for assistance, and in priority need, it must secure interim accommodation pending determination of what further duties may be owed. That said, the existence of the relief duty does not displace this obligation.

The relief duty ordinarily lasts for a period of 56 days, unless it is brought to an end earlier on one of the statutory grounds. These include:

- the applicant securing suitable accommodation available for at least six months;
- the applicant's refusal of a suitable offer of accommodation;
- a deliberate and unreasonable failure to co-operate with a step in the Personalised Housing Plan, following the required warning and notice procedure; or
- a referral to another local authority on the basis of local connection, where the statutory conditions are met.

Any decision to bring the relief duty to an end must be notified to the applicant in writing. The notification must set out the reasons for the decision, identify the statutory basis relied upon, and explain the applicant's right to request a review under section 202.

In practice, the relief stage often can present operational difficulty. From a legal perspective, however, the focus remains upon whether the local authority has taken reasonable steps on the evidence and has complied with the procedural structure imposed by the statute. If that statutory structure is not properly followed, decisions to end the relief duty are open to challenge.

2.3 The Main Housing Duty (s.193)

The main housing duty is regarded as the highest level of statutory protection under Part VII. It arises where the local authority is satisfied that the applicant:

- is homeless;
- is eligible for assistance;
- has a priority need;
- is not intentionally homeless; and
- is not to be referred to another local authority under the local connection provisions.

When these conditions are met, section 193 requires the local authority to secure that accommodation is suitable and available for occupation by the applicant and, if necessary, their household. A local authority cannot refuse to accept or perform the duty by reference to resource pressures, operational constraints, or local housing scarcity. Those factors may affect how the duty is performed, but they do not dilute the duty itself.

The statutory framework allows flexibility in the means by which the duty is discharged. In practice, a local authority may meet section 193 by securing social housing, continuing temporary accommodation pending a suitable settled offer, or discharging the duty by a suitable offer of accommodation in the private rented sector where the statutory conditions for a private rented sector offer are met. That said, the technical requirements for discharging the main housing duty by a private rented sector offer are strict. In *Norton v Haringey LBC* [2022] EWCA Civ 1340 the Court of Appeal confirmed that section 193 imposes a series of requirements, each of which must be satisfied before the duty ends. The offer letter must inform the applicant in writing of every matter specified in section 193(7AB). A failure to include the prescribed information means the duty has not been lawfully discharged. Local authorities should check offer letters against the full terms of section 193(7AB) before they are made.

Regardless of the route adopted, the legal requirement remains the same: the local authority must secure accommodation that is suitable.

It follows that suitability lies at the centre of section 193. By virtue of section 206, any accommodation secured in performance of a homelessness duty must be suitable, taking account of the applicant's particular circumstances. Suitability is not limited to physical condition alone, it also includes factors such as affordability, size and arrangement, location, accessibility, and the practical consequences for the household. That said, local authorities are expected to consider factors such as schooling, medical treatment, employment, and support arrangements where they are relevant to whether the placement is suitable. Suitability is also not a one-off assessment; where circumstances change, or where temporary arrangements extend over time, the local authority ought to keep suitability under review and respond lawfully to material developments.

The main housing duty can be brought to an end only in the circumstances prescribed by statute. In practice, common examples include acceptance of a suitable final offer, refusal of a suitable final offer (with the statutory consequences that follow), the applicant ceasing to be eligible for assistance, or other defined termination events. Any decision that ends, discharges, or materially affects the section 193 duty must be communicated in writing, must explain the reasons in clear terms, and must set out the applicant's right to request a review under section 202.

The statutory scheme expects the local authority to reach lawful decisions, based on adequate inquiries and supported by evidence, and to perform the duty through a process that remains transparent, reviewable, and compliant with the structure of Part VII.

2.4 Interim Accommodation (s.188)

Section 188 of the Housing Act 1996 imposes an immediate accommodation duty where the local authority has reason to believe that an applicant may be homeless, may be eligible for assistance, and may have a priority need.

Once the section 188 duty arises, the local authority ought to secure accommodation forthwith. The duty continues until the local authority has completed its inquiries under section 184 and has notified the applicant of a lawful decision. It is evident that interim accommodation cannot lawfully be withheld on the basis that inquiries are incomplete, that evidence is outstanding, or that the local authority considers the application to be weak.

Interim accommodation may take a number of recognised forms. Common examples include:

- **Emergency accommodation**, such as hotels or bed-and-breakfast accommodation, typically used at the point of first approach where no immediate alternative is available;

- **Hostels or other temporary accommodation**, including accommodation provided by housing associations or commissioned providers, often with shared facilities;

- **Self-contained temporary accommodation**, such as properties leased by the local authority from the private sector for short-term use.

Although interim accommodation is, by definition, temporary, it remains subject to the statutory requirement of suitability. Such accommodation should be safe, reasonably suitable for the applicant's household, and capable of meeting basic living needs. For families with children, extended use of bed-and-breakfast accommodation is subject to strict statutory limits, and local authorities must take active steps to secure more appropriate arrangements within the prescribed timeframe.

Further, local authorities are required to exercise care in accommodation placement decisions. Repeated moves, placements far from an applicant's established area, or accommodation that disrupts schooling, medical treatment, or support arrangements should be avoided. Where out-of-borough placement is necessary, the local authority ought to consider the individual circumstances of the household, record the reasons for the decision, and keep the placement under review.

Perhaps unsurprisingly, the section 188 duty does not end informally or by default. Interim accommodation can be brought to an end only when the local authority has reached and notified a lawful decision on the homelessness application, or where the applicant otherwise ceases to be entitled to accommodation under the statutory scheme. Any decision to withdraw or change interim accommodation must be communicated clearly and with reasons.

Section 188 operates as a core safeguard within Part VII. It ensures continuity of accommodation during the inquiry stage and prevents the statutory process itself from leaving applicants to immediate homelessness while their legal position is being determined. The section 188 duty is explored further in Chapter 9.

2.5 Ending Duties Lawfully

Each homelessness duty under Part VII can be brought to an end only in the circumstances prescribed by statute. A local authority's duties do not end by assumption, by administrative convenience, or simply because time has passed. A local authority should therefore approach "ending" decisions as formal legal decisions, reached on an identified statutory basis and capable of withstanding review.

To end a duty lawfully, a local authority should:

- identify clearly which duty is being ended;
- confirm that a statutory ground for ending that duty applies on the facts found;
- provide a written notification setting out reasons and the applicable review rights; and
- retain clear, contemporaneous records showing the evidence relied upon and the reasoning process.

In practice, the most common errors arise where case handling drifts into informal closure: for example, treating a duty as having "expired" without reference to the statutory criteria, failing to provide the required notice in writing, or attempting to end duties verbally during a telephone call or office appointment. Those approaches are, in essence, unlawful because they bypass the statutory structure and deprive applicants of the right to understand, and if necessary challenge, the basis on which the local authority says its obligations have come to an end.

The applicant should be able to ascertain, at any point, which duty the local authority accepts is currently owed, what steps are being taken (including any steps set out in a Personalised Housing Plan), and what events or decisions might lawfully bring the duty to an end. Similarly, where a local authority decides that the statutory conditions for ending a duty are met, the reasons should be set out with sufficient clarity to show how the legal test has been applied to the facts found.

2.6 Fair Process and Transparency

Given decisions under Part VII determine access to statutory assistance and accommodation, the process by which those decisions are reached should be fair, open, and transparent. Procedural fairness is a legal requirement that governs how a local authority exercises its homelessness functions at every stage.

In practice, fairness requires clear and consistent communication. Local authorities should explain the purpose of inquiries, the information being sought, and the reasons for any delay. By the same token, applicants should be given a genuine opportunity to provide relevant material and/or representations, to respond to adverse findings, and to correct misunderstandings before decisions are finalised. In circumstances in which the local authority relies on information obtained from third parties or internal sources that is adverse to the applicant's case, the substance of that material should be disclosed and the applicant given an opportunity to respond.

Any decision letters should:

- set out the material facts found and the evidence relied upon;
- explain how the relevant statutory rules and legal tests have been applied to those facts;
- state clearly the decision reached and the duty (if any) accepted; and
- identify the applicant's right to request a review, including the applicable time limits.

As such, decision letters that provide conclusions without explaining the reasoning, or that fail to identify the statutory basis for the decision, undermine the applicant's ability to seek a review and can expose the local authority to challenge. What can be said, however, is that clear documentation serves a dual function. Firstly, it enables applicants to understand the basis of the decision and, where appropriate, to exercise their statutory rights. At the same time, it may protect decision-makers by demonstrating that the correct legal framework has been applied in a reasoned way.

For these purposes, fair process and transparency ensure that homelessness duties are exercised in accordance with statute, that decisions are capable of being challenged, and that the local authority can account for the way in which it has applied Part VII in any individual case. The growing use of technology and artificial intelligence in homelessness decision-making raises further questions about transparency and fair process, which are considered in Chapter 12.

PART TWO

CORE STATUTORY TESTS

The statutory scheme governing homelessness operates through five core legal tests. Each test serves a distinct purpose, but none should operate in isolation. The tests shape the decision-making process, determining both whether an applicant is entitled to assistance and, if so, what form that assistance must take. Before any housing duty can arise, the local authority must work through this framework in respect of every applicant. It is the mechanism by which local authorities ensure that decisions are lawful, consistent, and procedurally fair.

These tests are sometimes regarded as technical or overly complex. In reality, they are not designed as barriers to assistance. They reflect Parliament's recognition that the duty to protect individuals from homelessness must be balanced against the obligation on local authorities to manage public resources responsibly. Each test asks a discrete legal question. Considered together, they determine the full extent of an applicant's entitlement.

- Eligibility asks who, as a matter of law, is entitled to seek housing assistance. The focus here is on immigration status and habitual residence.

- Homelessness examines whether the applicant has accommodation available to them and, if so, whether it is reasonable for them to continue to occupy it.

- Priority need identifies those whose circumstances place them at particular risk, and who therefore require a higher level of protection.

- Intentional homelessness considers whether the loss of accommodation resulted from a deliberate act or omission by the applicant.

- Local connection determines which local authority is responsible for providing assistance.

These five tests are the foundation of homelessness decision-making. Each test should be addressed, in the proper order, and resolved before any substantive housing duty can arise. Each of the following chapters addresses one of these tests, setting out the statutory basis, the applicable legal standards, and the issues that arise most frequently in practice.

CHAPTER THREE

ELIGIBILITY AND IMMIGRATION STATUS

Eligibility represents the first and most fundamental of the statutory tests in homelessness law. It operates as the gateway through which every applicant must pass before any substantive duty can arise. This threshold question determines whether an individual has any entitlement, at all, to housing assistance, whether temporary or permanent. It is placed at the intersection of housing and immigration law. It is beyond the scope of this book to address every aspect of immigration law, and the contents which follows is confined to those elements necessary to understand eligibility in the homelessness context. The aim is to identify and explain those parts of immigration law most relevant to homelessness decision-making. Eligibility is technically demanding and the consequences of error are immediate, and errors at this stage often have consequences that are immediate and severe. A single error may exclude a person who is lawfully resident from all statutory protection.

3.1 Statutory Basis

The legal framework governing eligibility for homelessness assistance is primarily contained in sections 185 and 186 of the Housing Act 1996, read together with the Allocation of Housing and Homelessness (Eligibility) (England) Regulations 2006, as amended, and Chapter 7 of the Homelessness Code of Guidance for Local Authorities. These rules establish the boundary between those who may access the homelessness system and those who are excluded from it by reason of immigration or residence status.

Furthermore, eligibility operates as a preliminary filter. Persons who are subject to immigration control are ineligible for homelessness assistance unless they fall within one of the categories expressly prescribed as eligible under regulation 5 of the 2006 Regulations. Persons who are not subject to immigration control may nevertheless be excluded where they fail to satisfy the habitual residence requirement. These inquiries are conceptually distinct but closely linked, and in practice they should be addressed in a structured and careful manner.

First, the local authority must establish the applicant's nationality and immigration status, including the nature of any leave to remain or enter and the conditions attached to it. Secondly, where eligibility is not excluded by immigration status, the local authority ought to consider whether the applicant is habitually resident in the United Kingdom ("UK"), the Channel Islands, the Isle of Man, or the Republic of Ireland. This means that only where eligibility is established can the local authority move on to assess homelessness, priority need, intentional homelessness, and local connection.

The statutory framework changes regularly, particularly in response to shifts in immigration policy and the consequences of EU withdrawal. Given both the complexity of the regime and the gravity of the consequences that arise from an adverse decision, eligibility determinations require legal precision and an informed understanding of current law, rather than a reliance on customs, assumptions, or outdated practice.

3.2 British and Irish Citizens

British citizens are not subject to immigration control and are therefore commonly eligible for homelessness assistance as of right. In most cases, proof of eligibility will be straightforward and readily established through providing a passport, birth certificate, or other citizenship documentation.

In the event formal documentation is unavailable, however, as may occur in cases involving rough sleeping, domestic abuse, or the loss or destruction of documents, local authorities are required to act reasonably. Applicants should be provided a reasonable opportunity to obtain replacement documentation, and decision-makers should be prepared to consider credible secondary evidence where appropriate. Local authorities should be wary of an approach which treats the absence of documentary proof as determinative, without further enquiry. This risks unlawfully obstructing access to the statutory scheme.

Irish citizens continue to benefit from the Common Travel Area arrangements, which long predate the UK's membership of the European Union and operate independently of it. These arrangements support reciprocal rights of residence and access to services between the UK and Ireland. For the purposes of homelessness assistance, Irish citizens should therefore be treated in the same manner as British nationals.

Any assessment of habitual residence in relation to an Irish citizen ought to be approached with care. Habitual residence is not a minimum-period requirement and should not be deployed as a proxy for nationality. That said, where there is clear evidence that a person's presence in the UK is purely temporary or transitory, then habitual residence will likely become in issue. Habitual residence will be explained in more detail later through this chapter.

3.3 Persons Subject to Immigration Control

A central threshold within the homelessness eligibility framework is whether the applicant is a "person subject to immigration control" within the meaning of section 185 of the Housing Act 1996. Section 185 provides that certain persons subject to immigration control are ineligible for homelessness assistance unless they fall within categories prescribed by the Allocation of Housing and Homelessness (Eligibility) (England) Regulations 2006. The concept is defined by reference to section 115 of the Immigration and Asylum Act 1999 and generally includes individuals who require leave to enter or remain in the UK but do not possess it, or whose leave is subject to conditions restricting access to public funds.

The eligibility framework operates in two stages. First, the local authority should determine whether the applicant is a person subject to immigration control. If the applicant is not subject to immigration control, they will normally be eligible for homelessness assistance provided that they satisfy the habitual residence test. Secondly, if the applicant is subject to immigration control, the local authority ought to consider whether they fall within one of the prescribed classes of persons who are treated as eligible for assistance under the 2006 Regulations.

This statutory structure reflects Parliament's intention that immigration status should work as a threshold gateway to homelessness assistance. However, as the later sections of this chapter demonstrate, the application of these provisions can be complex, particularly in cases involving EU Settlement Scheme status, refugee protection, victims of trafficking, or mixed households. Local authorities should therefore consider eligibility inquiries carefully and ensure that decisions are based on a correct understanding of both immigration status and the relevant eligibility regulations.

3.4 EEA and Swiss Nationals (Post-Brexit)

The legal position of EEA and Swiss nationals has changed fundamentally following the UK's withdrawal from the European Union. The former regime of free movement no longer applies, and eligibility for homelessness assistance now depends upon domestic immigration status, most commonly that granted under the EU Settlement Scheme.

Individuals granted settled status, which confers indefinite leave to remain, are eligible for homelessness assistance, subject to the habitual residence test and the other statutory criteria applicable to all applicants. In the event an applicant holds settled status under the EU Settlement

Scheme, local authorities are generally entitled to rely upon the Home Office decision granting that status when assessing eligibility, provided that the applicant continues to hold that status.

However, the position of holders of pre-settled status is more complex. Pre-settled status does not, of itself, confer eligibility for homelessness assistance under Part VII of the Housing Act 1996. To put it another way, to establish eligibility, a person with pre-settled status must demonstrate the existence of a qualifying right to reside of a type recognised under retained EU law. The Court of Appeal held in *Fertré v Vale of White Horse District Council* [2025] EWCA Civ 1057 that pre-settled status is a gateway status only. It does not confer a directly effective right to reside, and an applicant who holds no qualifying right to reside, such as being economically active or self-sufficient, remains ineligible for homelessness assistance under Part VII.

In practice, this will ordinarily require the applicant to show that they are a worker or self-employed person, that they possess a permanent right of residence, or that they are the primary carer of a child in education where the child's other parent is, or was, exercising EU Treaty rights as a worker or self-employed person.

The housing eligibility rules applicable to pre-settled status holders broadly reflect the right-to-reside rules that apply in the context of means-tested welfare benefits. This means that the mere possession of pre-settled status, without a qualifying right to reside, will not ordinarily establish eligibility for homelessness assistance.

Recent developments have emphasised that local authorities should also consider the UK's obligations under the EU Withdrawal Agreement and the EU Charter of Fundamental Rights when assessing eligibility for certain EU nationals. In particular, where refusal of homelessness assistance would leave an applicant unable to meet their most basic housing needs, local authorities should consider whether such refusal would create a real risk of a breach of the applicant's right to human dignity protected by Article 1 of the EU Charter.

The Court of Appeal in *Secretary of State for Work and Pensions v AT* [2023] EWCA Civ 1307 indicated that individuals protected by the Withdrawal Agreement may rely upon Charter rights where necessary to avoid such outcomes. In that sense, this means that a person with pre-settled status who lacks a qualifying right to reside may nevertheless require homelessness assistance where the absence of support would expose them to destitution or an inability to meet their most basic needs.

Similarly, the Homelessness Code of Guidance reflects this approach. If a local authority determines that homelessness assistance is required in order to avoid a breach of Charter rights, the applicant should be treated as eligible for homelessness assistance until the statutory duty ends or the circumstances giving rise to the Charter risk change.

Section 45 of the Border Security, Asylum and Immigration Act 2025 provides that all EU, EEA and Swiss nationals, and their family members, who hold status under the EU Settlement Scheme are to be treated as having rights under the Withdrawal Agreement for as long as they hold that status, whether or not they were exercising treaty rights at the end of the transition period. As a result, such persons may rely upon Charter rights, including the right to human dignity under Article 1, when seeking assistance necessary to avoid destitution.

In the event a pre-settled status holder is found not to have a qualifying right to reside, the local authority should nevertheless consider the individual circumstances of the case and should not apply blanket exclusions. In cases where eligibility is unclear but the applicant appears homeless and may be in priority need, interim accommodation under section 188 of the Housing Act 1996 ought to be considered pending resolution of the eligibility question. When a person is ultimately found ineligible, the local authority should still consider whether duties arise under other statutory regimes, including the Children Act 1989 or the Care Act 2014, and a local authority ought to remain mindful of its obligations under the European Convention on Human Rights.

In practice, local authorities should consider whether the applicant has access to alternative means of meeting their basic needs, including lawful employment, support from family or friends, or other sources of assistance. In the circumstance where such support is absent and the applicant faces an inability to meet their most basic housing needs, the risk of a Charter breach may arise and careful consideration is required.

Charter Eligibility Following *SSWP v AT*

The interaction between the EU Settlement Scheme, the Withdrawal Agreement and homelessness eligibility has become increasingly significant following the Court of Appeal's decision in *Secretary of State for Work and Pensions v AT* [2023] EWCA Civ 1307. The decision indicated that individuals within the scope of the Withdrawal Agreement may rely upon the EU Charter of Fundamental Rights where necessary to prevent a breach of fundamental rights.

In homelessness cases, this issue commonly arises where a person with pre-settled status does not possess a qualifying right to reside under the domestic eligibility regulations but would otherwise be left unable to meet their most basic needs. Article 1 of the Charter protects the right to human dignity. If refusal of homelessness assistance would expose an applicant to destitution or the inability to secure basic shelter, local authorities should consider whether such refusal would create a real risk of a breach of that right.

That being said, local authorities should consider whether the applicant has any realistic access to accommodation, employment, welfare benefits, or family support. In the circumstance where no such support exists and the applicant faces street homelessness or extreme deprivation, the Charter may require that homelessness assistance be provided.

If a local authority concludes that assistance is required to avoid a Charter breach, the applicant should be treated as eligible for homelessness assistance while that risk persists. Eligibility may cease if the circumstances giving rise to the risk change.

Zambrano Carers

A further category that may arise in practice concerns so-called "Zambrano carers". These are third-country nationals who derive a right to reside from their role as primary carer of a British citizen child who would otherwise be compelled to leave the United Kingdom if the carer were required to depart. Zambrano carers are not eligible for homelessness assistance, and this has been the settled position.

Where a Zambrano carer presents to a local authority without settled status, the local authority will not be able to accept a homelessness duty towards them directly. However, the British citizen child retains their own rights as a UK national, and the practical consequences for that child of any refusal of assistance must be carefully considered. If refusal would effectively compel the child to leave the United Kingdom alongside the carer, that is a relevant factor bearing on the local authority's wider public law obligations, and a bare refusal without any engagement with those consequences is likely to be difficult to defend.

In practice, the most important step a professional can take when advising a Zambrano carer is to examine their immigration status with particular care and, where status is unclear or an application is outstanding, to ensure specialist immigration advice is obtained as a matter of urgency. A successful application for settled status transforms the position entirely and opens the door to a full homelessness application. Until that status is established, the homelessness route is not available, and advice should be directed towards regularising immigration status rather than pursuing a homelessness application that the local authority has no power to accept.

3.5 Refugees and Humanitarian Protection

Applicants granted refugee status, humanitarian protection, or indefinite leave to remain are eligible for homelessness assistance. In addition, the 2006 Regulations prescribe further classes of persons who are to be treated as eligible, including individuals granted leave to remain as victims of trafficking or modern slavery, as well as certain other categories of limited leave with recourse to public funds, including, for example, those granted Unaccompanied Asylum-Seeking Child leave, leave under the Ukraine Schemes, the Migrant Victims of Domestic Abuse Concession, Hong Kong BN(O) visas, and leave granted on family or private life grounds under Article 8 of the European Convention on Human Rights.

By contrast, a person whose leave to remain is subject to a "no recourse to public funds" condition will ordinarily be ineligible for homelessness assistance unless that condition has been lifted.

It should be noted that newly recognised refugees often face a sharp transition when asylum support ends, typically after a short move-on period. It is therefore necessary that homelessness applications made at this stage should be treated as urgent, and local authorities should act promptly to secure interim accommodation where required. In fact, close liaison with asylum support providers is vital to avoid gaps in procedure and to ensure that responsibility transfers lawfully from one statutory regime to another.

3.6 Mixed Households

Modern family life frequently gives rise to mixed households comprising of individuals with differing immigration and eligibility statuses. Common examples include British citizen children living with parents who hold limited leave to remain, or households in which one partner is eligible for assistance while another is not.

In the event the principal applicant is eligible, the household should ordinarily be treated as a single unit for the purposes of homelessness assistance, notwithstanding the presence of ineligible family members. When the principal applicant is ineligible but another household member, most commonly a child, is eligible in their own right, the local authority should consider whether duties arise independently to that person. It will often be unreasonable, and potentially unlawful, to require the separation of close family members, particularly where children are involved.

Such cases frequently give rise to duties under the Children Act 1989 alongside the homelessness regime. Local authorities should therefore approach mixed-household cases with particular care and ensure effective cooperation between housing services and children's social care.

3.7 Habitual Residence

The habitual residence requirement is a further threshold condition, intended to ensure that homelessness assistance is directed towards those who are genuinely settled in the UK. In order to establish that an applicant is habitually resident in the UK, a local authority will ordinarily rely on a range of factual indicators drawn from the applicant's circumstances as a whole. These commonly include: (i) evidence of actual residence in the UK, including its length, continuity, and general nature; (ii) the applicant's accommodation arrangements, whether settled or informal; (iii) employment, economic activity, or other practical steps taken to live in the UK; (iv) family, social, and community ties; and (v) the consistency between the applicant's stated intentions and their conduct. The focus of the inquiry is whether the applicant has established the UK as their genuine home for the time being, as opposed to having been present for a particular period without any settled basis of residence.

Bearing that in mind, the concept is not defined in statute, and its application depends on a fact-sensitive evaluation rather than the application of inflexible rules. What can be said, however, is that while general principles are well understood, there remains considerable scope for disagreement at the margins, particularly in cases involving recent arrivals, returns following periods abroad, or applicants whose living arrangements are unsettled. The House of Lords held in *Nessa v Chief Adjudication Officer* [1999] 1 WLR 1937 that habitual residence requires both voluntary residence for a settled purpose and an appreciable period of time. The requisite period is not fixed and will vary depending on the circumstances. By way of illustration, there is no minimum period of residence required to establish habitual residence, yet mere intention to remain is insufficient without supporting factual evidence. Conversely, relatively short periods of residence may suffice where the quality and practicality of the arrangements demonstrate that residence has become settled and habitual in nature.

When an applicant has arrived in, or returned to, the UK within the previous two years, it will generally be necessary for the local authority to make further inquiries. In cases of an applicant's return, the central question is often whether the applicant is resuming a former period of habitual residence. In practice, relevant considerations may include the length of prior residence in the UK, the reasons for leaving and returning, the duration of absence, and whether the applicant retained a centre of interest here. Temporary or occasional absences do not necessarily break habitual residence where ties to the UK have been maintained. For new arrivals, the assessment turns on whether residence has moved beyond the transient and become settled in practice.

Local authorities' decisions on habitual residence should be reached by reference to evidence and clear reasoning, rather than an assumption or generalisation. Factors such as nationality, immigration status, or length of stay alone are not determinative. Instead, applicants should be given a proper opportunity to explain their circumstances and to provide relevant information. If the assessment is not approached in this way, there is a real risk that the threshold test will be applied incorrectly, with the result that an applicant may be wrongly excluded from the statutory scheme.

3.8 Special Categories: Armed Forces, Victims of Trafficking and Domestic Abuse

Certain categories of applicant retain eligibility notwithstanding restrictions that might otherwise arise from immigration status. Members of the UK Armed Forces and their family members benefit from specific protections intended to ensure that service-related mobility does not result in exclusion from homelessness assistance on discharge or transition.

Further to this, individuals recognised as victims of trafficking or modern slavery may be granted discretionary leave to remain with access to public funds and therefore eligibility for homelessness assistance. Victims of domestic abuse granted leave under specific Home Office concessions similarly retain eligibility during the currency of that leave.

Finally, cases involving these groups ought to be handled with particular care. Applicants may lack documentation, may be reluctant to disclose abuse, or may be concerned about potential immigration consequences. In such cases, priority should be given to the applicant's safety and welfare, and that should be reflected in the way the local authority carries out its inquiries.

3.9 Procedure and Evidence

The local authority must make such inquiries as are necessary to establish eligibility. This includes examining an applicant's immigration status and the rights attached to it. Decision-makers will ordinarily verify status using the Home Office's digital "View and Prove" service, while also considering physical documentation where available.

That said, when immigration status becomes unclear, local authorities may seek clarification from the Home Office, including through NRPF Connect where access is available.

In that sense, when eligibility is uncertain but the applicant appears homeless and may be in priority need, interim accommodation under section 188 should be provided pending clarification. Any decision that an applicant is not eligible should be communicated clearly in writing, identify the legal basis for the conclusion, and inform the applicant of their right to request a review under section 202 of the Housing Act 1996.

3.10 Summary

Eligibility is central to the homelessness framework. It operates as the legal threshold which determines whether an applicant may access the system of statutory protection at all. Its assessment requires accuracy, cultural awareness, and a current understanding of immigration law and policy, given the significant and often irreversible consequences which result from an adverse decision. Proper application of the eligibility criteria ensures that homelessness assistance is confined to those who fall within the statutory scheme.

Conversely, where eligibility is misunderstood or misapplied, there is a real risk that individuals whom the legislation was expressly designed to protect may be excluded from assistance altogether. Such errors may result not merely in administrative injustice, but in destitution and street homelessness for applicants and outcomes which the statutory scheme sought to prevent. Eligibility is therefore a central question, requiring careful judgment and a proper application of the law to the facts of the individual case.

CHAPTER FOUR

WHAT COUNTS AS HOMELESSNESS

Homelessness, in its legal sense, encompasses far more than the image of an individual sleeping rough on the streets. It extends to circumstances in which accommodation exists only in name, where it is insecure, unsafe, or so fundamentally inadequate that it cannot reasonably be regarded as a home. The statutory definition is intentionally broad, reflecting Parliament's recognition that homelessness is not a single or uniform condition, but a spectrum of housing insecurity shaped by social, economic, and personal factors. It may describe a family forced to move nightly between friends' sofas, an individual sleeping in a vehicle for lack of alternatives, a survivor of abuse fleeing their home in fear, or a tenant remaining in accommodation so compromised that continued occupation would pose a serious risk to health or safety.

Homelessness law asks not merely whether a person has a roof, but whether the accommodation they have is one they can reasonably be expected to occupy. This chapter examines the statutory meaning of homelessness under the Housing Act 1996, the evidential standards governing homelessness inquiries, and the principles which guide local authorities in the interpretation and application of the statutory scheme.

4.1 Definition and Reasonableness

The principal statutory definition of homelessness is found in section 175 of the Housing Act 1996. A person is homeless if they have no accommodation available to them, whether in the United Kingdom or elsewhere, or if they have accommodation but it is not reasonable for them to continue to occupy it.

Availability is not assessed by reference to the applicant alone. Section 176 of the Act provides that accommodation is only available if it is available for occupation by the applicant with any person who normally resides with them as a member of their family, or any other person who might reasonably be expected to reside with them. Where accommodation cannot usually be occupied by the whole household, the applicant is homeless regardless of whether they themselves could return or remain.

The concept of reasonableness is central to the statutory framework and requires an evaluative judgment which cannot be reduced to rigid rules or formalistic criteria.

Nevertheless, the assessment of reasonableness is grounded in the facts of the individual's case. It requires local authorities to reasonably take into account the reality of the applicant's circumstances, taking into account factors such as physical safety, health, affordability, the condition and security of the accommodation, and the personal and household context within which occupation takes place. The courts have consistently made clear that homelessness is not confined to the absence of physical shelter. A person may retain legal possession of accommodation and yet be homeless where the conditions of occupation, taken as a whole, render continued residence unreasonable.

The Court of Appeal held in *Lomax v Gosport BC* [2018] EWCA Civ 1846 that where a disabled applicant's circumstances are being compared against the general housing conditions in the area under section 177(2), the PSED requires sharp focus to be applied at each stage of that comparison. The reviewing officer must identify the applicant's disability and its extent, assess the likely effect of that disability on the applicant's ability to remain in the accommodation, identify the applicant's particular accommodation needs arising from the disability, compare those needs against the needs of non-disabled people in the area, and consider whether the applicant requires more favourable treatment as a result. A reviewing officer who attaches significant weight to general housing scarcity without first carrying out that analysis will not have complied with the PSED.

Situations in which accommodation may be unreasonable to occupy include, but are not limited to, circumstances where the applicant faces a real risk of violence, serious harassment, or intimidation within or in the vicinity of the home; where severe disrepair, damp, mould, infestation, or structural instability have rendered the property unsafe or injurious to health; where overcrowding is so extreme that it gives rise to demonstrable risks to physical or mental wellbeing; or where the cost of the accommodation is such that the applicant cannot meet ordinary living expenses while maintaining occupation.

The Court of Appeal held in *Rowe v Haringey LBC* [2022] EWCA Civ 1370 that the concepts of reasonableness to continue to occupy under section 175(3) and suitability under section 210 are distinct and are dealt with separately in the statute. However, depending on the facts, factors relevant to one assessment may also be relevant to the other.

Local authority inquiries are ought therefore to be contextual and fact-sensitive. The correct question is not whether it is physically possible for an applicant to remain in their accommodation, but whether it is reasonable, in all the circumstances, to expect them to do so. That assessment should be undertaken from the perspective of a reasonable person in the applicant's position, taking proper account of vulnerability, lived experience, and the cumulative impact of adverse conditions. As such, where continued occupation cannot reasonably be expected, homelessness is established for the purposes of the Act.

4.2 Threatened Homelessness

Section 175(4) of the Housing Act 1996 provides that a person is threatened with homelessness where it is likely that they will lose their accommodation within 56 days. This definition reflects the deliberate shift towards prevention and early intervention introduced by the

Homelessness Reduction Act 2017, and it marks a departure from earlier approaches which required applicants to wait until homelessness had materialised.

Once the risk of homelessness has materialised such that loss of accommodation is both real and imminent, the statutory prevention duty is triggered. This may arise in a wide range of circumstances and is not confined to formal eviction proceedings. Common examples include the service of a valid notice seeking possession, the making of a possession order, the withdrawal of permission to occupy by a family member or friend, or the impending discharge from hospital, prison, asylum accommodation, or other institutional settings where accommodation will no longer be available.

As outlined in Chapter 2, the statutory emphasis on the prevention duty imposes a proactive and forward-looking obligation on local authorities. It requires timely and proper communication with applicants, constructive efforts to resolve housing difficulties before they escalate, negotiation with landlords where appropriate, and coordination with welfare, health, and support services. Similarly, delay until eviction or actual loss of accommodation is inconsistent with the preventive purpose of the legislation and risks undermining the protective intent of the statutory scheme.

4.3 Domestic Abuse and Violence

Domestic abuse remains one of the most significant and distressing causes of homelessness. The statutory framework recognises unequivocally that no person should be expected to remain in accommodation where continued occupation would expose them to violence or abuse. Section 177 of the Housing Act 1996 provides that it is not reasonable to expect a person to occupy accommodation if it is probable that this will lead to domestic violence or other abuse. The Supreme Court held in *Yemshaw v London Borough of Hounslow* [2011] UKSC 3 that 'domestic violence' in section 177(1) of the Housing Act

1996 is not confined to physical contact. It includes physical violence, threatening or intimidating behaviour and any other form of abuse which, directly or indirectly, may give rise to the risk of harm. Where it is probable that such conduct will occur, it is not reasonable for the applicant to continue to occupy the accommodation. The person is automatically homeless on that basis, and questions of local housing conditions or shortages do not affect the position.

The concept of domestic abuse should now be understood in light of the statutory definition contained in section 1 of the Domestic Abuse Act 2021. This definition is deliberately broad and encompasses physical violence, sexual abuse, threatening behaviour, coercive or controlling conduct, economic abuse, emotional abuse, and psychological harm. Such abuse may be perpetrated by a current or former partner, a family member, or another individual with whom the applicant has a close personal relationship.

With this in mind, where an applicant cannot safely remain in their accommodation due to domestic abuse, they are homeless as a matter of law. Local authorities ought to respond promptly and with appropriate sensitivity. S188 accommodation should be secured promptly where required, confidentiality ought to be maintained throughout the process, and applicants should not be encouraged to return to or reconcile with a perpetrator. By the same token, where children are involved, safeguarding duties arise concurrently under the Children Act 1989 and should be addressed alongside the homelessness application.

Local authorities should take a trauma-informed approach in these cases. Survivors may approach local authorities without documentation, may be reluctant or unable to disclose the full extent of the abuse, or may fear the consequences of seeking assistance with public authorities. Housing officers should facilitate access to specialist domestic abuse services and ensure that support is accessible, culturally appropriate, and responsive to the individual needs of the applicant.

4.4 Unsuitable or Unsafe Accommodation

Homelessness may also arise where accommodation, albeit technically available, is unsuitable for occupation. Section 175 of the Housing Act 1996 requires local authorities to look beyond questions of legal entitlement and consider the actual suitability of accommodation in practice.

Accommodation may be unsuitable where it suffers, for example, from serious disrepair, persistent damp or mould, infestation, lack of essential facilities, or environmental conditions that pose a risk to health or safety. Similarly, overcrowding, lack of privacy, and the impact of the living environment on an applicant's physical or mental health are also relevant considerations. In some cases, medical or professional evidence will demonstrate that continued occupation of a property would exacerbate illness or disability to an extent that renders it unreasonable.

It is important to remember that affordability is also an integral part of the reasonableness assessment. In order to determine whether accommodation can reasonably be continued to be occupied, local authorities are required to examine affordability as a substantive component of the assessment. This will ordinarily involve consideration of a range of factors, including: (i) the applicant's actual income from employment or benefits; (ii) the level of rent and service charges payable; (iii) unavoidable household expenditure such as utilities, food, and transport; and (iv) any particular financial pressures arising from health needs, disability, or family composition. The underlying objective is to establish whether the cost of the accommodation leaves the applicant unable to meet ordinary living needs, such that continued occupation would be unreasonable.

Affordability assessments are long-established but can be difficult to apply in practice. It is neither sufficient nor lawful for a local authority to rely on generic benchmarks, standardised assumptions, or formulaic conclusions. Whilst it may be possible to assess affordability by reference to income and outgoings in broad terms, experience demonstrates that individual circumstances frequently introduce variables which materially affect the outcome. By way of example, applicants may incur atypical costs linked to medical treatment, caring responsibilities, debt repayment, or fluctuating income. These factors may not be apparent from headline figures alone, yet they may decisively affect whether accommodation is realistically sustainable.

In practice, assertions of unsuitability on affordability grounds require proper inquiry. Local authorities are required to make proper and proportionate inquiries and, where appropriate, to obtain supporting material such as financial breakdowns, environmental health input, photographic evidence, or medical information. The test remains objective, but it must be applied to the facts of the individual case. The ultimate question is whether a reasonable person, properly informed of the applicant's financial position and living conditions, could fairly be expected to continue to occupy the accommodation in question.

4.5 Exclusions and Temporary Absences

The absence of a current address does not, of itself, render a person homeless for the purposes of the statutory scheme. The Housing Act 1996 recognises that certain temporary absences do not extinguish an individual's accommodation. A person temporarily residing in hospital, in custody, serving in the armed forces, or accommodated in another institutional setting will not ordinarily be homeless where they retain accommodation which remains available and reasonable for occupation upon release or discharge.

The position changes where accommodation ceases to be available in practice. This may occur where rent arrears accrue during a period of absence, where a landlord re-lets the property, or where a relationship underpinning the right to occupy breaks down. Similarly, a person staying elsewhere on a short-term basis will remain housed only where they retain both the legal right and the practical ability to return.

In such cases, the assessment should focus on the continuing availability of the accommodation and the reasonableness of occupation, rather than on physical presence alone.

4.6 Proof and Evidence

Homelessness inquiries ought to be investigative rather than adversarial in nature. Section 184 of the Housing Act 1996 requires local authorities to make such inquiries as are necessary to satisfy themselves whether an applicant is homeless or threatened with homelessness and, if so, what duties are owed.

In practice, applicants ought to be given a proper opportunity to explain their circumstances and to provide information or evidence in support of their application. In such circumstances, relevant material may include tenancy agreements, notices seeking possession, possession orders, correspondence from landlords or lenders, police reports, medical evidence, or statements from family members, friends, or support agencies. The absence of formal documentation is not determinative alone. Where documentary evidence cannot reasonably be obtained, credible oral evidence ought to still be considered and evaluated as part of the overall assessment.

Any decision reached must be communicated in writing and must set out the local authority's findings of fact, the evidence relied upon, and the reasoning which leads to the conclusion reached. Formulaic or opaque reasoning will not suffice. In fact, transparency in decision-making is a substantive legal requirement, enabling applicants to understand decisions affecting their housing position and providing an essential safeguard of accountability.

That being said, where doubt remains, particularly in cases involving vulnerability or credible indications of imminent homelessness, local authorities ought to act with caution. Interim accommodation should ordinarily be provided pending completion of inquiries where appropriate. A failure to adopt this protective approach risks unlawful inaction and leaves applicants to avoidable harm in circumstances where the statutory scheme is expressly designed to provide early and effective protection.

4.7 Summary

Homelessness, as a matter of law, encompasses a wide range of circumstances, extending beyond those who are sleeping rough to include individuals who are occupying accommodation in conditions which no reasonable person could properly be expected to endure. The statutory definition extends well beyond rough sleeping, nor does it turn solely on formal legal rights or the existence of a tenancy agreement. Rather, it is grounded in considerations of safety, stability, and the availability of accommodation which it is reasonable for the applicant to continue to occupy. While section 175 of the Housing Act 1996 provides the statutory foundation for the definition, the operative question is one of reasonableness applied to the facts of the individual case.

Local authorities are therefore required to carry out a holistic assessment of each application and have regard to all relevant circumstances, which may include exposure to violence or threats of violence, insecurity of tenure, serious disrepair, overcrowding, affordability, and the suitability of the accommodation for the household concerned. The statutory scheme requires local authorities to act preventively and responsively, addressing risks at an early stage and engaging with applicants in a manner which is timely, careful, and sensitive, particularly where the household includes survivors of abuse, children, or other vulnerable persons.

The homelessness legislation exists to provide assistance. Its purpose is to ensure that those who qualify have access to accommodation that is genuinely suitable. The test of homelessness is therefore both legal and factual. It requires an evaluation of whether the applicant has accommodation which they can reasonably be expected to regard as their home. In reality, where that question is answered in the negative, the applicant is homeless and the statutory duties arise.

CHAPTER FIVE

PRIORITY NEED

The concept of priority need occupies a central position within the statutory framework governing homelessness assistance. It operates as the mechanism by which local authorities determine which eligible and homeless applicants may be owed the full housing duty under Part VII of the Housing Act 1996. Whilst the preliminary tests of eligibility and homelessness establish whether an applicant may enter the statutory scheme at all, the assessment of priority need determines the scope and intensity of the duty which follows. In this respect, it reflects Parliament's recognition that, in a context of finite public resources, certain categories of applicant face a materially greater risk of harm if left without accommodation.

Priority need therefore determines which eligible and homeless applicants may be owed the full housing duty. Its purpose ensures that assistance is directed towards those who, by reason of their personal circumstances, are least able to manage the consequences of homelessness. The distinction between applicants who fall within the priority need categories and those who do not is often decisive. Those applicants found to be in priority need may be entitled to settled accommodation or, at the very least, longer-term temporary housing, whereas those who fall outside the definition may be owed only limited duties of advice and assistance.

5.1 Statutory Categories

The statutory foundation for priority need is contained in section 189 of the Housing Act 1996. That statute identifies categories of persons who are to be treated as having a priority need for accommodation as a matter of law. These categories reflect Parliament's assessment that certain individuals and households face a greater risk of harm if left without accommodation and therefore require enhanced protection within the homelessness framework.

Section 189(1) provides that a person has a priority need if they fall within one or more of the following categories:

- a pregnant woman, or a person with whom a pregnant woman resides or might reasonably be expected to reside;
- a person with whom dependent children reside, or might reasonably be expected to reside;
- a person who is vulnerable as a result of old age, mental illness, physical disability, or other special reason, or a person with whom such a vulnerable person resides or might reasonably be expected to reside;
- a person who is homeless or threatened with homelessness as a result of an emergency, such as flood, fire, or other disaster;
- a person who is homeless as a result of being a victim of domestic abuse, this category having been inserted into the primary legislation by the Domestic Abuse Act 2021.

However, these primary statutory categories do not stand alone. They have been supplemented by secondary legislation, most notably the Homelessness (Priority Need for Accommodation) (England) Order 2002, which extends priority need to additional groups. These include most 16- and 17-year-olds (subject to limited exceptions), care leavers aged 18 to 20 who were previously looked after by a local authority, and persons who are vulnerable as a result of having served in the armed forces, having been imprisoned or detained, or having fled violence or threats of violence.

Importantly, section 189 does not operate as a closed or exhaustive code. Even where an applicant does not fall squarely within one of the expressly defined categories, they may nonetheless be found to be in priority need under section 189(1)(c) by reason of vulnerability arising from an "other special reason". The courts have considered what may constitute an other special reason on a number of occasions. It is not confined to physical or mental illness and may include, for example, severe social isolation, a history of institutional care, or a combination of personal circumstances which, in aggregate, render the applicant significantly less able to cope with homelessness than an ordinary person. The question is always one of fact and degree, assessed by reference to the applicant's individual circumstances.

Local authorities are therefore required to apply the statutory categories rigorously but fairly, having regard to the primary legislation, relevant statutory instruments, applicable statutory guidance, and binding case law. Although the priority need assessment is structured by defined legal categories, it remains an evaluative exercise which calls for reasoned judgment rather than mechanical classification, and which should be rooted in a careful appraisal of the applicant's individual circumstances.

5.2 Vulnerability and the Hotak Test

The modern interpretation of "vulnerability" derives from the decision of the Supreme Court in *Hotak v Southwark LBC* [2015] UKSC 30, which overruled the earlier and more restrictive approach taken in *Pereira v Camden LBC* (1998) 31 HLR 317.

In *Hotak*, the Supreme Court held that an applicant is "vulnerable" for the purposes of section 189(1)(c) if, when homeless, they would be significantly more at risk of harm than an ordinary person in need of accommodation. Crucially, the "ordinary person" is a comparator drawn from the general population of those facing homelessness, rather than from an assumed baseline of street homelessness. As a result, local authorities ought to consider whether the applicant's personal characteristics, physical or mental illness, disability, or social circumstances render them less able to cope with the consequences of homelessness.

It is important to appreciate that the assessment is necessarily factual and holistic. It requires an evaluation of various factors including the applicant's capacity to manage the ordinary demands of daily life if homeless, including securing shelter, maintaining health, obtaining food and sanitation, and accessing medical or social support. While the presence of family or professional support may be relevant, it is only so insofar as that support is effective, reliable, and realistically available. Accordingly, local authorities should consider both the applicant's inherent capacities and the practical reality of any external assistance upon which reliance is placed.

Vulnerability may also arise where an applicant faces a number of difficulties which, viewed in isolation, might not establish vulnerability, but which in combination create a significantly greater risk of harm if homeless.

The Supreme Court in *Hotak* also made clear that vulnerability is a legal concept, not a medical diagnosis. Medical evidence is often important and may be highly persuasive, but it is not determinative. The local authority's task is to reach a lawful conclusion on vulnerability, informed by expert evidence but not dictated by it. The correct question remains whether, taking everything into account, the applicant's condition and circumstances render them significantly less able to fend for themselves than an ordinary person if homeless.

In practice, the *Hotak* approach requires local authorities to articulate clearly both the comparator being applied and the factual basis for any conclusion reached. Decision-makers ought to identify the ordinary person facing homelessness against whom the applicant is being assessed, set out the applicant's specific characteristics and circumstances, and explain why those factors do or do not give rise to a significantly increased risk of harm. Conclusory statements that an applicant can "cope" with homelessness are insufficient unless supported by analysis of how they would manage in reality. Where reliance is placed on support from family members, friends, or services, the local authority should explain why that support is considered reliable and effective, rather than merely theoretical. A lawful decision will set out a clear evaluation of risk, based on evidence, and will show that the local authority has given due regard to the applicant's circumstances in their entirety, rather than reducing vulnerability to a diagnosis or a list of conditions.

5.3 Medical and Social Factors

In determining vulnerability, local authorities should consider both medical and non-medical evidence. Physical illness, mental disorder, learning disability, addiction, and sensory impairment may all bear upon an applicant's ability to withstand homelessness. When such issues are raised, a local authority should ordinarily seek medical advice; however, it must not delegate its decision-making function to the medical assessor.

As the courts have repeatedly emphasised, the local authority, not the medical assessor, is the statutory decision-maker (*Cramp v Hastings BC* [2005] EWCA Civ 1005). The local authority ought to therefore evaluate all evidence and provide compelling reasons for accepting or rejecting particular opinions. Thus, a conclusion that a person is "fit for independent living" does not preclude a finding of vulnerability where homelessness would materially worsen their condition or expose them to serious risk.

Where a reviewing officer proposes to prefer one body of medical evidence over another, they must explain why. The Court of Appeal held in *Guiste v Lambeth LBC* [2019] EWCA Civ 1758 that a reviewing officer who preferred the views of medical advisers who had not examined the applicant over a more detailed and authoritative expert report, without explaining why, acted irrationally and in breach of the principles of fair decision-making. The duty to engage with conflicting evidence is not discharged merely by obtaining a medical opinion. Where a reviewing officer departs from the more authoritative expert evidence, a rational explanation is required.

Equally, social and environmental factors may be of decisive importance. The absence of family support, social isolation, limited English proficiency, cognitive impairment, or exposure to discrimination may substantially impair an individual's ability to cope with homelessness. For example, an elderly applicant who is recently bereaved and without community ties may be significantly less able to navigate homelessness services than a younger person in good health with established local networks. Conversely, a medical condition may be mitigated by strong, reliable support systems. The assessment ought to therefore address both individual characteristics and the practical reality of available assistance.

For this reason, local authorities should avoid formulaic reasoning. Vulnerability is not a label conferred by diagnosis alone, but a contextual assessment of functional capacity in the circumstances of homelessness. The duty under section 184 of the Act to make "such inquiries as are necessary" requires that all relevant medical, social, and personal evidence be properly investigated, weighed, and recorded before any conclusion is reached.

Where an applicant has mental health difficulties, local authorities should consider engaging with community mental health teams or other relevant services to obtain a fuller picture of the applicant's circumstances and support needs. A failure to make those inquiries where they are obviously called for may itself render a priority need decision unlawful.

5.4 Families, Young People, and Care Leavers

Households that include dependent children, and pregnant women, are automatically in priority need by operation of section 189(1)(a) and (b). This reflects Parliament's intention to protect children from the consequences of homelessness and aligns with the wider duties imposed by the Children Act 1989, in particular section 17. Consequently, where homelessness arises in such circumstances, local authorities should liaise promptly with children's services to ensure that the needs of both parents and children are addressed appropriately.

Further, young people aged 16 or 17 are also deemed to have priority need unless they fall within the specific care duties of children's services. In addition, the 2002 Priority Need Order extends priority status to care leavers aged 18 to 20 who were previously looked after, fostered, or accommodated by a local authority.

These provisions recognise that young people leaving care or institutional settings often lack the social, emotional, and financial resources necessary to manage independently. Nevertheless, such priority is not indefinite. Once a care leaver turns 21 and is not in full-time education or demonstrably vulnerable, automatic priority ceases, though vulnerability under section 189(1)(c) may still arise on the ordinary principles.

Local authorities should therefore ensure that effective inter-departmental protocols are in place. The courts have made clear that failures of cooperation between housing and children's services may amount to unlawful administrative action.

5.5 Victims of Domestic Abuse and Other Special Groups

As outlined earlier in this Chapter, victims of domestic abuse now have priority need as a matter of primary statute by virtue of the amendment to section 189(1) introduced by the Domestic Abuse Act 2021. This means that an applicant who is homeless as a result of domestic abuse has priority need without the need to establish vulnerability separately. The 2002 Order separately covers persons who are vulnerable as a result of having fled violence or threats of violence more broadly, and the statutory question in those cases remains whether the applicant is vulnerable as a result of that experience rather than whether the violence occurred.

Where the domestic abuse category under section 189(1) applies, local authorities should not impose an additional requirement to demonstrate vulnerability. The statutory protection is engaged by the fact of domestic abuse causing homelessness, and the assessment should proceed on that basis. Local authorities ought to conduct an objective assessment of the applicant's circumstances, taking account of the risk of further harm and the psychological impact of past abuse, when determining what duties are owed and what accommodation is suitable.

Similarly, persons who are vulnerable as a result of having served in the armed forces, or having been imprisoned or detained, fall within the scope of the Order. In such cases, vulnerability may arise from institutionalisation, post-traumatic stress, mental illness, or difficulties reintegrating into civilian life. Local authorities should be alert to these risks and seek appropriate supporting evidence, such as service records, medical reports, or probation documentation, where relevant.

5.6 Evidence, Inquiry, and Reasoning

The determination of priority need engages the local authority's duty under section 184 of the Housing Act 1996 to make "such inquiries as are necessary" into the applicant's circumstances. Decisions must be founded on adequate evidence.

Applicants should be informed of the nature of the inquiries being made and given a fair opportunity to provide relevant material. Where medical evidence is obtained, applicants should ordinarily be given the opportunity to comment upon it before a decision is finalised. That said, conflicting expert opinions ought to be resolved through reasoned evaluation rather than by defaulting to one opinion without explanation. Local authorities are required to give clear and intelligible reasons for their findings, explaining why certain evidence has been accepted and other evidence rejected.

In contrast, a failure to carry out adequate inquiries or to take proper account of medical or factual evidence will commonly lead to a decision unlawful on public law grounds. The burden does not rest on the applicant to prove priority need, but on the local authority to conduct lawful inquiries and reach a rational conclusion on the balance of probabilities. Decisions should be expressed in clear language, citing relevant statutory provisions and case law where appropriate. That being said, formulaic conclusions such as "not vulnerable" or "fit for homelessness" are inadequate and risk successful challenges by way of review or appeal.

Decision makers should also note that the relief duty under section 189B applies regardless of priority need, as addressed in Chapter 2. Priority need becomes determinative at the stage where the local authority is considering whether the main housing duty under section 193 arises. Advisers should therefore ensure that the absence of priority need does not result in the applicant being turned away without the relief duty being properly considered and discharged.

5.7 Summary

Priority need is the statutory mechanism through which the Housing Act 1996 may allocate the full homelessness duty to those at greatest risk of harm. Section 189 defines core categories, including families with children, pregnant women, persons homeless due to emergency, persons homeless as a result of domestic abuse and those vulnerable for special reasons, while the 2002 Order and subsequent case law expand and refine the scope of protection.

The modern test of vulnerability, as articulated in *Hotak*, requires an assessment of whether the applicant would be significantly more at risk of harm than an ordinary person if homeless. That assessment ought to be holistic, evidence-based, and supported by clear reasoning. The equality duty under section 149 of the Equality Act 2010 applies to that assessment and must be considered where the applicant has a relevant protected characteristic.

Ultimately, the law requires local authorities to inquire properly and to justify their conclusions. Priority need is not a moral judgment, but a legal threshold. When properly applied, it ensures that assistance is directed where the statutory criteria are met and withheld where they are not, and maintains the protective purpose of the homelessness regime.

CHAPTER SIX

INTENTIONAL HOMELESSNESS

Intentional homelessness is one of the more contentious aspects of the statutory framework of homelessness law. It functions as a legal mechanism for distinguishing between those whose loss of accommodation results from circumstances beyond their control and those whose conduct has directly and deliberately caused that loss. However, while the term "intentional" may suggest moral culpability, the test is a legal one, not an ethical judgment. The decision-maker is not concerned with whether the applicant is to be blamed in a colloquial sense, but whether the statutory criteria for intentionality are satisfied on the evidence. Section 191 of the Housing Act 1996 provides the operative definition, and it governs both the structure of the inquiry and the discipline of reasoning expected of local authorities.

6.1 Statutory Definition and Purpose

Section 191(1) of the Housing Act 1996 provides that:

"A person becomes homeless intentionally if he deliberately does or fails to do anything in consequence of which he ceases to occupy accommodation which is available for his occupation and which it would have been reasonable for him to continue to occupy."

Four constituent elements must therefore be established:

- A deliberate act or omission by the applicant;

- Availability, in that the accommodation was available for occupation for the applicant and any person who normally resides with them or might reasonably be expected to do so;

- Causation, in that the act or omission led to the loss of accommodation;

- Reasonableness, meaning that it would have been reasonable for the applicant to continue to occupy that accommodation.

All four limbs should, in the ordinary course, be satisfied before a finding of intentional homelessness can lawfully be made. The statutory purpose is to prevent the manipulation of the homelessness scheme—for example, the surrender of suitable accommodation in order to trigger rehousing duties—yet the test is not to be applied as a punitive device, still less as a moral sanction. It requires careful attention to the applicant's state of mind, the voluntariness and context of their actions, and the practical reality of continued occupation in their circumstances.

Moreover, section 191 itself contains an important internal safeguard. An act or omission occurring in good faith by a person who was unaware of any relevant fact is not to be treated as deliberate, a rule which reinforces that intentionality is concerned with controllable choice rather than misfortune, mistake, or ignorance. Section 191(2) provides that an act or omission in good faith by a person who was unaware of any relevant fact shall not be treated as deliberate. The Court of Appeal confirmed in *O'Connor v Kensington and Chelsea RLBC* [2004] EWCA Civ 394 that the subsection contains two distinct requirements: good faith, and ignorance of a relevant fact. Both must be addressed separately. Subsuming one within the other, or treating them as a single composite assessment, is a misdirection in law. An applicant who shuts their eyes to an obvious fact or risk cannot claim good faith, and the protection of the subsection will not apply.

Conversely, section 191(3) extends the intentionality provisions to cover collusive arrangements. Where an applicant deliberately procures another person to take steps resulting in the loss of accommodation — such as arranging for a landlord to serve a notice to quit — a finding of intentional homelessness may be made on that basis. The provision prevents applicants from circumventing the statutory test by engineering homelessness through a third party rather than by their own direct act, and local authorities should consider it where the circumstances suggest that the loss of accommodation was contrived rather than genuine.

Although the inquiry is evaluative, it is not open-ended. The local authority bears the burden of establishing, on the balance of probabilities, that the applicant's homelessness was the deliberate and foreseeable result of conduct meeting the statutory definition, and a lawful decision will usually be one which shows, with clarity, how each element has been addressed rather than asserted.

Professionals should also note that section 196 of the Housing Act 1996 provides a parallel definition of intentionally threatened with homelessness, which mirrors section 191 but applies at the prevention stage. Where an applicant is found to have deliberately brought about the threat of homelessness, the prevention duty will not arise in the same way as it would for an applicant who faces threatened homelessness through no fault of their own. The same structured analysis of deliberateness, causation, and reasonableness applies at the prevention stage as it does when assessing intentional homelessness itself.

6.2 Deliberate Act or Omission

The first element, deliberateness, requires that the applicant's conduct relied upon was a conscious, voluntary act or omission carried out with an appreciation of its likely consequences. Illustrations include, though are not limited to:

- voluntarily leaving accommodation without securing a suitable alternative;
- refusing to pay rent or mortgage instalments despite having the financial means to do so;
- selling or transferring property without reasonable cause or forward planning; or
- breaching tenancy obligations intentionally, leading to eviction.

In that sense, deliberateness is rarely proved by mere descriptions; it is proved, if at all, by the evidence. A local authority should be satisfied that the applicant understood the relevant facts and accepted the probable outcome of their conduct. However, what appears "voluntary" on the surface may be vitiated by context. An applicant's conduct may be driven by mental illness, coercion, domestic abuse, addiction, or a genuine misunderstanding of legal or factual circumstances, and in such cases it cannot straightforwardly be characterised as deliberate for the purposes of section 191.

A person who leaves accommodation to escape violence, for example, does not act intentionally within the meaning of the statute albeit the act of leaving is voluntary in the literal sense; likewise, non-payment of rent resulting from benefits delay, administrative failure, or genuine inability to meet essential living costs cannot simply be treated as a deliberate default. The question is thus not merely whether the applicant acted or failed to act, but whether the conduct was within their control and undertaken with sufficient knowledge of the facts that make the conduct properly describable as a deliberate cause of homelessness.

In practice, decision-makers need to approach deliberateness with precision. They should identify what the relevant act or omission was, what the applicant knew at the time, what choices were realistically open to them, and whether the outcome relied upon was a probable consequence of the conduct said to be deliberate.

6.3 Availability of Accommodation

The second element requires that the accommodation which the applicant is said to have deliberately vacated or lost was, at the material time, available for their occupation within the meaning of section 176 of the Act. As explained in Chapter 4, accommodation is only available for an applicant's occupation if it is available for occupation by them and any other person who normally resides with them as a member of their family, or any other person who might reasonably be expected to reside with them.

The availability requirement is a substantive condition, and its omission from a decision letter will ordinarily render that decision subject to challenge on review or appeal. A local authority that identifies a deliberate act, establishes causation, and concludes that continued occupation would have been reasonable, but fails to address whether the accommodation was available within the statutory meaning, has not completed the inquiry the statute envisaged.

In practice, the requirement often arises in household cases. Accommodation nominally held by an applicant, or to which they had a legal right of occupation, may nonetheless fail the availability test if it was not realistically available to the whole household. A property that could not physically accommodate dependent children, a partner excluded by conduct or court order, or a family member whose presence was essential but whose occupation was not possible, will not satisfy section 176 merely because the applicant themselves could have stayed. The question is whether the accommodation was genuinely available to everyone who needed to live there, not to the applicant alone.

6.4 Causation and Reasonableness of Continued Occupation

The third and fourth statutory elements, causation and reasonableness, should be analysed distinctly, though in practice they frequently interact. The local authority must determine (i) whether the applicant's deliberate conduct caused them to cease to occupy the accommodation, and (ii) whether, at the relevant time, it would have been reasonable for them to continue to occupy it. The ultimate objective of this exercise is to demonstrate that the applicant deliberately acted or failed to act in a way that caused them to cease to occupy accommodation that was available and reasonable to continue to occupy.

Although causation is a long-established element of the intentional homelessness test, its application is not without difficulty. It is beyond the scope of this book to examine every factual scenario in which causation may be disputed. What can be said, however, is that while the legal framework is well settled, its practical application frequently gives rise to error. In particular, there is a recurring tendency to elide dissatisfaction with accommodation, disputes about suitability, or anticipated future loss with the statutory requirement that the applicant has actually become homeless as a result of their conduct.

Legally speaking, causation requires a properly evidenced causal link between the applicant's deliberate conduct and the homelessness. It is not enough that the conduct forms part of the background narrative; rather, the question is whether it was an operative cause of the loss of accommodation. Put simply, and without reducing the importance of this test, the local authority should ask whether, but for the deliberate conduct, the applicant would have remained accommodated. In the event the answer is uncertain, or where later events have overtaken the original sequence, a finding of intentional homelessness may not be lawful.

In *Din v Wandsworth LBC* [1983] 1 AC 657 the House of Lords held that the relevant date for determining intentional homelessness is the date on which the applicant left the accommodation, not the date of the local authority's decision. That principle was confirmed by the Supreme Court in *Haile v London Borough of Waltham Forest* [2015] UKSC 34, which added an important qualification. There must be a continuing causal connection between the earlier deliberate act and the homelessness existing at the date of decision. The inquiry looks backwards from that date to identify the operative cause of the present homelessness. Where a supervening event would have rendered the applicant homeless in any event, the causal connection with the earlier act is broken and a finding of intentional homelessness cannot stand.

In other words, an earlier deliberate act does not retain causal force because it sits somewhere in the history; if later events intervene so that the applicant would have become homeless in any event, the earlier act may be overtaken.

Whether intervening accommodation is sufficiently settled to break the chain of causation is a question of fact and degree, assessed as a whole having regard to all the circumstances of the individual case and the purposes of the legislation. In *Doka v Southwark LBC* [2017] EWCA Civ 1532 the Court of Appeal held that what an applicant must establish is a period of occupation which has, at its outset or during its term, a real prospect of continuation for a significant or indefinite period. The length of occupation is not conclusive. In *Bullale v City of Westminster Council* [2020] EWCA Civ 1587 the Court of Appeal confirmed that the assessment must take into account all relevant circumstances, including the nature and terms of the tenancy or licence, the expectations of the parties at the outset, whether the arrangement was commercial or personal, affordability, overcrowding, and the context in which the accommodation was obtained. A review officer who focuses on a single factor without engaging with the others will not have conducted a lawful assessment.

A causal chain may therefore be broken by an intervening event that becomes the effective cause of homelessness. Common examples include:

- a landlord's independent decision to recover possession for reasons unconnected to the applicant's conduct (such as sale, redevelopment, or occupation by a family member);

- the termination of occupation due to supervening conditions unrelated to the applicant's behaviour, including disrepair or damage rendering the accommodation uninhabitable;

- circumstances making continued occupation unsafe, such as violence, harassment, or exclusion;

  or

- changes in the applicant's circumstances such that homelessness now arises for reasons distinct from the earlier conduct.

Two recurring analytical "break points" are of particular importance.

Material change in circumstances (the material change test).
Even where an applicant's conduct contributed to an earlier loss of accommodation, the local authority needs to consider whether there has been a material change such that the earlier conduct is no longer the effective cause of the present homelessness. The inquiry is forward-facing: what has in fact caused homelessness at the time of the decision, rather than who might be thought responsible for earlier events.

Settled accommodation after the event (the settled accommodation test).
Where, following the alleged deliberate act, the applicant secures accommodation that is settled in reality, the causation analysis will ordinarily be reset. If the applicant later becomes homeless from that later accommodation, intentionality ought to be assessed by reference to the later loss, not by automatic reversion to earlier history. The question of what counts as "settled" is itself fact-sensitive and turns on the stability and reality of the arrangement, rather than the labels attached to it.

Reasonableness, by contrast, is an evaluative judgment governed by the principles set out in Chapter 4. Even where a deliberate act or omission is established and a causal connection could otherwise be drawn, a finding of intentional homelessness cannot lawfully be made unless, at the material time, it was reasonable to expect the applicant to continue to occupy the accommodation. This assessment is practical and fact-sensitive. It focuses on the conditions prevailing at the point of an applicant's departure and those reasonably foreseeable thereafter, rather than on generalised assumptions of suitability. The House of Lords held in *Birmingham v Ali and Moran v Manchester* [2009] UKHL 36 that the question of whether it is reasonable to continue to occupy accommodation is not confined to the present moment but incorporates a forward-looking element. Accommodation may be reasonable to occupy in the short term while ceasing to be reasonable to occupy in the medium or longer term. The assessment of reasonableness must therefore look ahead to the foreseeable future as well as to conditions at the date of decision.

This is particularly important in cases involving safety, serious disrepair, or genuine unaffordability. By the same token, where accommodation exposes an applicant to a real risk of violence or serious harassment, where conditions undermine basic habitability, or where the costs cannot be met without sacrificing essential living needs, an applicant leaving that accommodation may be a reasonable and proportionate response. In those circumstances, the statutory scheme does not appear to treat the resulting homelessness as intentional merely because the act of leaving was deliberate in the everyday sense.

A critical, and sometimes overlooked, component of the causation is the requirement that the applicant must have ceased to occupy the accommodation said to have been lost. Without cessation of occupation of that accommodation, the statutory chain cannot be completed. An applicant who remains in occupation of accommodation — including interim or temporary accommodation provided pursuant to statutory duties — cannot, as a matter of law, have become homeless intentionally from that accommodation. Given that, local authorities' assertions based on intention to leave, threats of eviction, or disagreement with conditions of occupation are insufficient substitutes for the statutory requirement of cessation.

In this sense, the local authority should conduct a structured, evidence-based analysis of all three elements—deliberate conduct, causation, and reasonableness—and a lawful decision will generally show (i) what facts have been found, (ii) why causation is established notwithstanding any intervening events (including material change or any period of settled accommodation), and (iii) why continued occupation would nevertheless have been reasonable.

6.5 Affordability and the Samuels Principle

The modern approach to affordability in intentional homelessness cases is governed by the Supreme Court's decision in *Samuels v Birmingham City Council* [2019] UKSC 28. The case concerned an applicant who had ceased paying rent due to a genuine shortfall between housing costs and available income, including welfare benefits. The Court held that a person cannot properly be found intentionally homeless where accommodation was not affordable once reasonable living expenses are taken into account.

Samuels establishes that affordability should be assessed realistically. Local authorities ought to examine the applicant's financial position in a detailed and evidence-based manner, including:

- household income and benefit entitlement;
- necessary living costs (including food, utilities, transport, and childcare);
- outstanding debts or essential liabilities where they bear upon subsistence; and

- rent and service charges.

In conjunction with this, the local authority should then determine whether the applicant could reasonably have been expected to meet rent payments without depriving themselves or dependants of basic necessities. The test is not whether the applicant might theoretically have prioritised rent above all other expenditure, but whether continued payment was realistically sustainable. In such a scenario, where the shortfall was unavoidable, non-payment cannot properly be treated as a deliberate act for the purposes of section 191. In that respect, *Samuels* reinforces a core distinction within the statutory scheme.

For that reason, local authorities should carry out affordability assessments carefully and demonstrate, in their reasoning, that they have properly applied the approach required by *Samuels*, rather than relying on generalised assertions that different budgeting choices could have been made.

6.6 Procedural Requirements and Evidential Standards

A finding of intentional homelessness gives rise to significant procedural safeguards. Under section 184 of the Housing Act 1996, the local authority should make "such inquiries as are necessary" before reaching its decision. It requires that relevant evidence be sought, assessed with care, and reasoned transparently in writing.

Likewise, applicants should be informed of the nature of the inquiries being undertaken and given a reasonable opportunity to respond. In practice, relevant material may include tenancy agreements, rent statements, notices, court orders, correspondence from landlords, bank records, benefit information, and medical or support evidence where it bears on deliberateness, capacity, coercion, or the reasonableness of remaining in the accommodation. Where disputes arise—whether about what was said, what was done, what was affordable, or what risks existed—the local authority needs to make findings of fact supported by evidence and should explain why one account has been preferred over another.

Accordingly, the decision letter should set out the reasoning process clearly, explaining how each statutory element—deliberateness, causation, and reasonableness—has been satisfied. As such, vague conclusions such as "the applicant made themselves homeless" are not adequate, particularly in cases where later events may have intervened, where affordability is disputed, or where safety concerns arise. Moreover, where the local authority relies on principles such as supervening events or affordability, it needs to demonstrate that it has understood and applied the relevant legal approach in substance, not merely by citation.

6.7 Consequences of a Finding of Intentional Homelessness

In the event an applicant is found to be intentionally homeless but is nevertheless in priority need, section 190(2)(a) of the Housing Act 1996 requires the local authority to secure accommodation for such period as it considers will give the applicant a reasonable opportunity to secure their own accommodation. This duty is temporary in nature and comes to an end once the local authority is satisfied that a reasonable opportunity has been provided.

In addition, section 190 imposes a continuing duty to provide advice and assistance to help the applicant secure accommodation. Whilst limited, this duty is enforceable and should be carried out conscientiously. It may include practical guidance on accessing private rented accommodation, negotiating with landlords, understanding benefit entitlement, and obtaining support from relevant agencies.

Applicants found intentionally homeless retain the right to request a review under section 202 of the Act and, if dissatisfied with a review decision, to appeal on a point of law to the County Court under section 204. These processes will be explained in later chapters.

6.8 Points to Note

Intentional homelessness represents a statutory boundary within the homelessness regime. The test, rooted in section 191 of the Housing Act 1996, requires a structured analysis of deliberate conduct, causation, and reasonableness. It is not a vehicle for moral condemnation, but a mechanism for ensuring that public assistance is distributed according to legal principle and administrative fairness.

In such circumstances, decisions in this area demand rigour and transparency. Local authorities should demonstrate that they have applied the statutory tests conscientiously, considered the relevant evidence—including financial, medical, and contextual material—and articulated clear reasoning in their decisions. *Samuels* reinforces the principle that inability, poverty, and necessity do not equate to intention, while cases such as *Haile* illustrate the importance of identifying the operative cause of homelessness and recognising when later events have overtaken earlier conduct.

Correctly applied, the test ensures that public assistance is available to those whose homelessness arises from circumstances beyond their control, while excluding only those whose homelessness is the foreseeable and deliberate product of their own conduct.

CHAPTER SEVEN

LOCAL CONNECTION AND REFERRALS

The statutory concept of local connection operates as the mechanism by which responsibility for homelessness applications is allocated between local authorities. Its function is administrative: to allocate responsibility between local authorities on the basis of established facts and ensure that applicants are assisted by the local authority with which they have the closest factual and practical association, and to prevent opportunistic applications to local authorities with which they have no genuine link. Proper application of these rules distributes responsibility fairly between local authorities and avoids arbitrary concentrations of demand.

Although the concept serves an organisational purpose, its determination nonetheless raises substantive legal questions relating to residence, employment, family relationships, and personal safety. Sections 198 and 199 of the Housing Act 1996 provide the statutory foundation for this allocation exercise, supplemented by the Homelessness Code of Guidance for Local Authorities and long-established administrative practice governing referrals between local authorities.

7.1 Statutory Framework and Purpose

The statutory starting point lies in section 198 of the Housing Act 1996, which provides that where a local authority is satisfied that an applicant is homeless and eligible for assistance, but has no local connection with its borough, it may refer the homeless application to another local authority where the applicant does have such a connection, provided that the applicant would not face a risk of violence in that other area.

Section 199(1) then defines the circumstances in which a person is to be regarded as having a local connection to a local authority. These are:

- normal residence in the area, of the person's own choice;
- employment within the area;
- family associations with persons who reside in the area and have done so for a significant period;

  or

- special circumstances giving rise to a particular connection.

These provisions establish a framework of objective criteria against which an applicant's factual circumstances should be assessed. The determination is not a matter of discretion or policy preference, but of evidence and fact. Importantly, the local connection test does not determine whether a homelessness duty arises, but rather which local authority is responsible for discharging it.

The policy rationale is straightforward. Each local authority bears primary responsibility for individuals with genuine ties to its district, thereby avoiding the concentration of demand in areas perceived to be more favourable or better resourced. Nevertheless, the statutory framework requires that the rules be applied lawfully, rationally, and with careful regard to the particular circumstances of each applicant, rather than through rigid or formulaic application.

Where an applicant has no local connection with any local authority, section 199(6) of the Housing Act 1996 provides that no referral can be made. In those circumstances, the local authority to which the application was made must retain responsibility and discharge whatever duties are owed. This situation arises in practice where applicants have moved frequently, have recently arrived in the country, or have spent extended periods in institutional settings without establishing residence of their own choice in any district. Local authorities should not attempt to refer such applicants on the basis of speculative or historical connections. The duty to assess and discharge the applicable obligations remains with the local authority to which the application was made. Applicants in this position should also be advised of their right to request a review of any local connection decision under section 202 of the Housing Act 1996, as addressed in Chapter 10.

7.2 Residence: Meaning and Duration

A local connection through residence requires that the applicant has lived in the area of their own choice and that such residence possesses a degree of permanence and stability. Residence which is compelled by external circumstances—such as imprisonment, hospitalisation, military service, or placement in accommodation under homelessness legislation—does not ordinarily amount to residence by choice for the purposes of section 199(1)(a).

Local authorities should therefore distinguish between voluntary residence forming part of an applicant's settled life, and conversely residence which is involuntary, institutional, or transient in nature. The central question is whether the applicant chose to live in the area as part of their ordinary pattern of life, rather than merely being present there by necessity or compulsion.

The Homelessness Code of Guidance indicates that residence of six months during the preceding year, or three years within the previous five, will generally constitute strong evidence of normal residence. These benchmarks are not determinative and should not be applied mechanistically. Ultimately, the assessment turns on the quality, continuity, and character of the residence rather than duration alone.

The House of Lords held in *Mohamed v Hammersmith and Fulham LBC* [2001] UKHL 57 that the normal residence limb of section 199(1)(a) is to be given its ordinary meaning — a place where, at the relevant time, the person in fact resides. Provided the residence was voluntarily accepted, the reason the person was there rather than elsewhere does not prevent it from being their normal residence. Interim accommodation provided under section 188 is capable of giving rise to a local connection on this basis. The House of Lords further held in *Al-Ameri (FC) v Kensington and Chelsea RBC* [2004] UKHL 4 that residence in accommodation provided under the NASS dispersal scheme is not residence of the applicant's own choice within section 199(1)(a), as the legislation required the provider to disregard any preference of the asylum seeker as to location.

Accordingly, local authorities should consider a range of factors, including:

- the nature and stability of the accommodation occupied;
- whether residence was interrupted by temporary or enforced absences;
- the applicant’s intentions regarding settlement in the district; and
- the extent to which genuine community links were established.

In practice, documentary evidence such as tenancy agreements, council tax records, utility bills, or school attendance records may assist in corroborating residence, albeit the absence of formal documentation is not necessarily conclusive where other credible evidence exists.

7.3 Employment and Family Associations

(a) Employment

A local connection may also arise through employment within the district. The employment need not be full-time, permanent, or salaried. Part-time work or self-employment may suffice provided that it is genuine and effective. Employment will generally be regarded as genuine where it forms part of the applicant's settled way of life, produces regular remuneration or income, and is not contrived for the purpose of establishing a local connection.

In assessing employment-based connections, local authorities should examine:

- the duration and regularity of the work;
- the location of the workplace in relation to the district;
- the nature of the employment, whether casual, seasonal, or ongoing; and
- whether the employment continues at the time of the homelessness application.

Employment taking place outside the district does not necessarily preclude a local connection where the applicant habitually travels to work from accommodation within the district, and the overall pattern of life is centred there.

(b) Family Associations

Section 199(1)(c) provides that a person may have a local connection through family associations within the district. This will typically include parents, adult children, or siblings who have resided in the area for a substantial period and with whom the applicant maintains genuine and ongoing contact. The Code of Guidance does not prescribe a fixed minimum period and local authorities should assess the duration and quality of the family member's residence in the district as a matter of fact, rather than applying a rigid numerical threshold.

The local authority should assess not only the existence of a familial relationship, but its practical significance. As such, occasional contact or estranged relationships will not ordinarily suffice. For applicants, relevant evidence may include correspondence, records of financial or practical support, or statements confirming regular interaction. The underlying rationale is to recognise the practical and emotional support available through family ties, which may render one local authority better placed to assist than another.

(c) Special Circumstances

Section 199(1)(d) operates as a residual category, allowing a local connection to be established by other special circumstances. This provision ensures flexibility within the statutory scheme and may encompass matters such as previous long-term residence, sustained community involvement, or the need for specialist medical or support services available only within the district.

The Court of Appeal held in *Hussaini v Islington London Borough Council* [2025] EWCA Civ 22 that a local connection exists where a person has a connection in real terms with a local authority's district by reason of one of the matters in section 199(1). When considering special circumstances under section 199(1)(d), a local authority may take into account whether an applicant needs to live in the district — the existence of such a need will support a connection, and its absence may make one less probable — but a local authority is not entitled to make it a threshold requirement. The fundamental question is always whether a local connection in real terms exists.

Bearing this in mind, its purpose is to prevent rigid application of the rules where an applicant's circumstances fall outside the standard categories but nonetheless demonstrate a genuine and substantive link.

7.4 Multiple Connections and Comparative Assessment

Applicants will frequently have connections with more than one district, particularly where patterns of employment, family life, or previous residence overlap. Section 199(2) expressly recognises this possibility and permits a finding that an applicant has a local connection with more than one local authority.

In such cases, responsibility is determined through inter-local authority negotiation, informed by administrative practicality and the relative strength of the competing connections. Local authorities should avoid a formulaic approach based solely on the length of time spent in each area. The correct inquiry is where the applicant's most substantial and enduring connection lies, assessed by reference to residence, employment, and family associations taken together.

7.5 Referrals Between Authorities

Where a local authority concludes that the applicant has no local connection with its district but does have such a connection elsewhere, and that no risk of violence would arise, it may initiate a referral under section 198(1). The referral process is governed by the Homelessness (Decisions on Referrals) Order 1998 and the accompanying procedures provided by the Local Government Association.

The referring local authority must:

- notify the applicant in writing of its intention to make a referral and the reasons for doing so;

- provide written notice to the receiving local authority setting out the applicant's circumstances, evidence of the alleged local connection, and confirmation that no risk of violence has been identified; and

- continue to secure interim accommodation pending determination of the referral.

The receiving local authority should, within the prescribed timeframe, either accept or dispute responsibility. Where a dispute arises, it is determined in accordance with the arrangements established under section 198(5) of the Housing Act 1996, which in practice are administered by the LGA's Inter-Authority Referrals Panel. The Panel's determinations are binding on both local authorities.

The statutory requirements of communication and record-keeping are strict. Failure to comply with the prescribed procedure renders a referral invalid, with the consequence that responsibility remains with the referring local authority.

Where a referral is being contemplated, section 184(4) of the Housing Act 1996 requires the local authority to notify the applicant in writing that it is considering making a referral, the reasons for that consideration, and the applicant's right to make representations. This notification is a mandatory procedural step and failure to provide it will ordinarily render any subsequent referral unlawful. Applicants should also be informed of their right to request a review of the local connection decision under section 202, as addressed in Chapter 10.

7.6 Violence and Safety Exceptions

Section 198(2) of the Housing Act 1996 imposes an absolute prohibition on referral where the applicant, or any person who might reasonably be expected to reside with them, would be at risk of violence in the district of the receiving local authority. This exclusion is mandatory. Once credible evidence of such risk exists, the referring local authority must retain responsibility for the homelessness application, irrespective of the strength of any local connection elsewhere.

For these purposes, "violence" is interpreted broadly and purposively. It includes not only physical assault and explicit threats, but also, following legislative developments, all forms of domestic abuse within the meaning of section 1 of the Domestic Abuse Act 2021. As discussed earlier in this book, particularly in Chapters 4 and 5, domestic abuse encompasses psychological abuse, coercive or controlling behaviour, economic abuse, and patterns of intimidation or harassment. These forms of harm are capable of rendering accommodation unsafe even in the absence of overt physical violence.

The relevance of domestic abuse within the local connection framework must be understood in light of its treatment elsewhere in the statutory scheme. As explained in Chapter 5, victims of domestic abuse may fall within priority need where vulnerability arises from the abuse itself, while Chapter 4 addresses the principle that accommodation is not reasonable to occupy where continued residence would expose an applicant to abuse or serious harm. The violence exception in section 198(2) operates consistently with those principles, ensuring that procedural allocation rules do not override substantive protections provided to those at risk.

In practice, local authorities are therefore required to adopt a cautious and protective approach. Any inquiries ought to be conducted sensitively, without requiring corroboration at the initial stage, and with due regard to the realities of disclosure in cases of abuse. The evidential threshold is one of credibility rather than proof beyond doubt. As such, a reasonable belief that a risk of violence or abuse exists is sufficient to preclude referral to another local authority. This approach reflects not only the statutory language, but also the local authority's wider public law obligations to safeguard life, prevent foreseeable harm, and avoid decisions which would expose applicants to further harm.

7.7 Interim Accommodation Pending Determination

Whilst a referral is under consideration, section 200(1) of the Housing Act 1996 requires the local authority that received the original homeless application to continue to secure interim accommodation. Responsibility does not transfer until the receiving local authority has formally accepted the referral.

This ensures that disputes about responsibility do not leave applicants without accommodation. The applicant's entitlement to accommodation persists throughout the referral process, and only once acceptance is confirmed by written notice does the duty pass to the receiving local authority. In practice, effective coordination between local authorities is essential, and any failure to maintain accommodation pending determination may amount to a breach of statutory duty.

7.8 Evidence, Record-Keeping, and Procedural Integrity

A local authority's decisions concerning local connection are heavily evidence-dependent. Local authorities should maintain comprehensive and contemporaneous records, including:

- chronologies of residence and employment;
- documentation or statements evidencing family associations;
- records of inter-local authority communications; and
- written notifications provided to the applicant at each procedural stage.

Clear record-keeping serves both transparency and accountability. It enables applicants to understand how decisions have been reached and provides the evidential foundation for defending those decisions on review or appeal. Such decision letters should identify the statutory rules applied, the evidence relied upon, and the reasoning leading to the conclusion.

A failure to document the decision-making process constitutes a procedural defect and may render a decision unlawful under established public law principles of rationality, fairness, and transparency.

PART THREE

PROCEDURE, DECISION-MAKING AND REMEDIES

Homelessness law is concerned not only with the substance of decisions, but with the manner in which those decisions are reached. The statutory framework governing homelessness assistance is deliberately procedural in character, reflecting Parliament's recognition that fairness, transparency, and accountability are not peripheral considerations, but integral to the lawful operation of the scheme. A person's entitlement to housing assistance means little if the process through which it is accessed is obstructed, delayed, or distorted by inadequate inquiry, defective reasoning, or poor administrative practice.

This part of the book therefore turns to the machinery of homelessness decision-making: the sequence of steps by which a request for assistance is transformed into a lawful outcome. It examines how applications are made and triggered, the scope and depth of the inquiries local authorities are required to undertake, the duties that arise at different procedural stages, and the mechanisms by which decisions may be challenged or corrected. It also addresses the standards of practice that can underpin the entire process, including record-keeping, communication, and the giving of reasons.

Procedure in homelessness law is not a formality; it is the means by which substantive rights are realised and protected. Each form completed, each inquiry pursued, each decision letter made, and each record maintained is a safeguard for the person the law is designed to protect.

CHAPTER EIGHT

MAKING A HOMELESSNESS APPLICATION

A homelessness application is the statutory medium by which an individual brings themselves within the statutory scheme contained in Part VII of the Housing Act 1996. It is the procedural trigger that converts an approach for assistance into a legally regulated process governed by defined duties, timeframes, and standards of decision-making. The legislation sets a deliberately low bar for what counts as an application, reflecting Parliament's intention that access to the homelessness framework should not be restricted by formality, technical language, or internal administrative arrangements.

The law makes clear that a homelessness application arises at the point when a local authority has reason to believe that a person may be homeless or threatened with homelessness. It does not depend upon the completion of a prescribed form, the making of an appointment, or the applicant's use of particular terminology. Any such approach to the local authority which, viewed objectively, raises the possibility of homelessness is sufficient to start the statutory scheme. From that point, the local authority's procedural obligations begin, and the inquiries undertaken will inform the assessment of the substantive duties discussed earlier in this book, including the prevention and relief duties set out in Chapter 2.

8.1 The significance of the initial approach

The initial approach to a local authority is legally significant because it marks the point at which the statutory homelessness framework is activated. In practice, applications frequently follow changes in housing, financial, or personal circumstances, including the expiry of a tenancy, relationship breakdown, loss of employment, or deterioration in health. From a legal perspective, however, the relevance of these circumstances lies in their effect: whether they give the local authority reason to believe that homelessness may exist or be imminent.

The framework governing the receipt of homelessness applications is contained principally in sections 183 and 184 of the Housing Act 1996, as amended by the Homelessness Reduction Act 2017. The statutory intention is to ensure that individuals who may be homeless or threatened with homelessness are able to access assistance promptly and without procedural obstruction. Accordingly, the application process is triggered by substance rather than form. An applicant need not understand that they are making a homelessness application, nor must they articulate their circumstances in legal terms. The duty arises from the information conveyed, not from the applicant's characterisation of it.

This low threshold is integral to the structure of the Act. Parliament deliberately rejected an approach under which homelessness ought to be conclusively established before assistance is offered. Instead, the legislation requires early and proper enquiries, so that the local authority can assess whether the prevention duty under section 195, or the relief duty under section 189B, may be owed, as explained in Chapter 2. As such, practices which delay or deflect the making of initial enquiries undermine the statutory scheme and are inconsistent with its preventive orientation.

8.2 The duty to take an application (sections 183–184)

Section 183 of the Housing Act 1996 imposes a duty on every local authority to consider applications from persons who appear to be homeless or threatened with homelessness. Once the local authority has reason to believe that homelessness may be an issue, the obligation to accept an application and to make inquiries under section 184 is triggered. This duty operates as a procedural gateway: it is the means by which the local authority assumes responsibility for investigating the applicant's circumstances within the statutory framework.

The threshold of reason to believe is intentionally low. Local authorities should not insist upon formal proof of homelessness before the duty arises. An applicant need not be sleeping rough, subject to a possession order, or in possession of eviction documentation. A report that accommodation is likely to be lost within 56 days, or that no accommodation is available for the immediate future, is sufficient for the duty to arise. The obligation arises upon the local authority's knowledge of facts capable of supporting the belief that homelessness may exist, not upon a concluded determination that it does.

Front-line staff therefore carry out a legally significant function. Information communicated to reception staff, customer service teams, or other departments of the local authority is capable of triggering the duty under section 183. A local authority cannot rely on internal administrative structures or departmental divisions to avoid its statutory obligations. Where relevant information is received by any part of the local authority, the duty to take an application and move to inquiry arises.

8.3 Inquiries and assessment

Once an application has been accepted, the local authority must make such inquiries as are necessary to determine what duty, if any, is owed to the applicant. Section 184 confers a wide discretion as to the scope and nature of those inquiries, but that discretion ought to be exercised in accordance with public law principles, including fairness, proportionality, and rational evaluation. The local authority's role at this stage is inquisitorial rather than adversarial. Its task is to establish the relevant facts, not to test the applicant's account as though in litigation.

The inquiries undertaken at this stage serve multiple purposes. They inform the local authority's assessment of eligibility, homelessness, priority need, intentionality, and local connection. They also provide the factual basis upon which the local authority determines whether the prevention duty under section 195 or the relief duty under section 189B is owed, as discussed in Chapter 2. The scope of inquiry should therefore be sufficient to allow those statutory duties to be identified and, where appropriate, discharged lawfully.

In practice, inquiries will commonly involve investigation of the applicant's accommodation history, household composition, financial circumstances, health, and support needs. The depth of inquiry required will vary. Where homelessness is self-evident, limited verification may be sufficient. Conversely, when facts are disputed or unclear, more detailed investigation will be required.

Procedural fairness requires transparency throughout the inquiry process. Where the local authority obtains information adverse to the applicant's case, it must disclose the substance of that information and give the applicant a reasonable opportunity to respond. This obligation arises from the common law duty to act fairly and applies irrespective of the source of the information. Each stage of the inquiry should be clearly recorded, with dates, summaries of discussions, and copies of relevant documents retained on the case file.

8.4 Personalised Housing Plans (PHPs)

The Homelessness Reduction Act 2017 introduced the Personalised Housing Plan as a central procedural component of the homelessness framework. The PHP operates as the practical link between the section 184 inquiries and the substantive prevention and relief duties described in Chapter 2. It is not a discretionary document, but a statutory requirement through which those duties are given practical effect.

The PHP ought to identify the factors contributing to the applicant's actual or threatened homelessness and specify the reasonable steps to be taken by both the local authority and the applicant to prevent or relieve it. In doing so, it reflects the local authority's assessment of whether the prevention duty under section 195, or the relief duty under section 189B, arises. The local authority remains responsible for ensuring that the steps included in the plan are reasonable, lawful, and capable of implementation.

In practice, such steps may include negotiation with landlords, assistance with rent arrears, referral to support services, or guidance on securing alternative accommodation. The plan needs to be specific and operational. Generic or aspirational steps are unlikely to satisfy the statutory requirement. The PHP should also be reviewed and revised where circumstances change, including changes affecting accommodation, income, household composition, or health. Treating the PHP as a static document is inconsistent with the statutory purpose and undermines the effective discharge of the prevention and relief duties.

8.5 Notification and communication of decisions

Once inquiries are complete, the local authority must notify the applicant in writing of its decision under section 184. The notification should set out the decision reached, the reasons for it, the duty owed (if any), and the applicant's right to request a review under section 202. This written notification is a substantive legal requirement and forms the foundation upon which any challenge may be brought.

It is an important point to note that decision letters should be properly reasoned. A bare conclusion that an applicant is intentionally homeless or not in priority need, without explanation, is legally insufficient. The local authority's reasoning should demonstrate how the statutory tests have been applied to the facts found and why particular conclusions have been reached. Where necessary, local authorities should take steps to ensure that the applicant understands the decision, including providing translation or explanation, and recording that this has been done.

For decision makers, properly reasoned decisions facilitate effective review and appeal by enabling errors of law or fact to be identified with precision. Clear communication supports lawful administration and reduces avoidable disputes.

8.6 Interim accommodation pending inquiries

Section 188 of the Housing Act 1996 imposes a duty to secure interim accommodation where the local authority has reason to believe that the applicant may be homeless, eligible for assistance, and in priority need.

Local authorities should adopt a cautious approach, and where uncertainty exists as to whether the criteria are met, the appropriate action is to secure accommodation pending resolution. Any accommodation provided must be suitable, having regard to household composition, medical needs, and identified risks.

The duty continues until a lawful decision under section 184 has been made and notified. Interim accommodation cannot lawfully be withdrawn simply because inquiries are ongoing or delayed. In fact, premature withdrawal of interim accommodation risks breach of a local authority's statutory duty and exposure to judicial review.

8.7 Repeat homelessness applications and fresh duties

An applicant is not barred from making a further homelessness application simply because a previous application has been refused or brought to an end. Part VII of the Housing Act 1996 imposes no numerical limit on applications, nor does it permit a local authority to refuse to entertain an application merely because an earlier decision has already been made. On the contrary, sections 183 and 184 impose a continuing obligation to respond where an applicant applies for assistance and the local authority has reason to believe that they may be homeless or threatened with homelessness.

Although where a further approach is made following the lawful conclusion of an earlier application, the local authority is entitled to consider whether the later approach amounts to a homelessness application at all. This does not involve revisiting the merits of the earlier decision. Instead, it requires a focused comparison between the facts as they were found at the point when the earlier application (or review) was finally determined, and the facts asserted in support of the later approach.

The governing principles were first articulated by the House of Lords in *R v Harrow LBC ex p Fahia* [1998] 1 WLR 1396, and subsequently applied to the Housing Act 1996 by the Court of Appeal in *Rikha Begum v Tower Hamlets LBC* [2005] 1 WLR 2103. Those leading authorities make clear that there is no general "threshold test" requiring an applicant to demonstrate a change of circumstances that might lead to a different outcome. The statutory duty to make inquiries arises unless the later approach is based on *precisely the same facts* as those which were known to, and accepted by, the local authority when the earlier application was finally disposed of.

The case law establishes a two-stage analysis:

At the first stage, the local authority must ask whether the later approach is an application at all. It will only fall outside Part VII if it is based on exactly the same factual matrix as the earlier application, disregarding allegations that are plainly fanciful or trivial. This is a narrow exception. The local authority is not entitled to carry out investigative inquiries at this stage, however brief or informal, in order to test the accuracy or sufficiency of the new assertions.

If the later approach discloses facts which, taken at face value, are not fanciful or trivial when compared with the facts as previously determined, it must be treated as a fresh application. The local authority then moves to the second stage, at which point the full statutory procedure applies. Then, inquiries must be undertaken under section 184, and interim accommodation should be considered in accordance with section 188 if the relevant criteria are met. There is no lawful "short cut" once the application has passed the first stage.

Fresh medical evidence frequently illustrates the distinction between these stages. Updated medical reports, new diagnoses, evidence of deterioration, or material not previously available may each amount to new facts for these purposes. Crucially, the comparison is not between what the applicant previously alleged and what is now alleged, but between the facts as *found* by the local authority in the earlier decision and the facts now asserted. Medical evidence that was previously rejected, discounted, or not considered at all cannot later be treated as if it had been accepted. Where fresh medical material is produced, the local authority should therefore consider whether it alters the factual landscape as previously determined.

By contrast, where an applicant merely repeats the same factual circumstances that were already accepted and determined, without advancing any genuinely new information, the local authority is not necessarily required to conduct a further full investigation or make a new decision. Even then, the local authority must still have proper regard to the approach to satisfy itself that no new facts have been raised. A blanket refusal to consider repeat approaches, or reliance on informal "non-statutory" inquiries, will very likely be unlawful.

This assessment is one of substance rather than form. Changes in accommodation, health, household composition, risk factors, immigration status, or local connection may each be capable of constituting new facts, depending on context. Local authorities should therefore approach repeat applications with care and record clearly the basis on which they conclude that an approach is, or is not, a fresh application. If doubt exists, the safer and legally better course is to accept the application and make inquiries in accordance with the statutory scheme.

CHAPTER NINE

TEMPORARY AND INTERIM ACCOMMODATION

Temporary accommodation occupies a central place within the statutory homelessness scheme. It is often the means by which the law provides immediate protection to individuals and families who would otherwise be without a place to live while inquiries are undertaken or duties continue. The statutory framework imposes clear legal standards governing when temporary accommodation should be provided, the conditions it must meet, and the manner in which placements must be reviewed and brought to an end.

It is a legal instrument through which local authorities discharge defined statutory duties. As such, the provision, location, affordability, and duration of temporary accommodation are all matters of law, subject to challenge where decisions fall outside the scope of what the legislation permits.

9.1 The function and purpose of temporary accommodation

Temporary accommodation represents one of the most significant operational components of the homelessness framework. It functions as the immediate mechanism by which protection is provided to applicants who cannot safely or reasonably remain where they are, and for whom the statutory scheme requires continuity of accommodation while duties are assessed or discharged.

In the field, temporary accommodation serves two interrelated purposes. First, it provides a lawful means of ensuring that applicants are not left without accommodation while inquiries are made or duties under the Act are ongoing. Secondly, it enables local authorities to comply with their statutory obligations under Part VII of the Housing Act 1996, as amended, in a manner that is consistent with the Homelessness Code of Guidance and wider public law principles.

In reality, the arrangement of accommodation alone is not sufficient. The statutory scheme requires that accommodation secured under homelessness duties should be suitable. As such where accommodation is unsafe, unaffordable, inappropriate for the household, or maintained without proper review, it may itself become unlawful. The duty to accommodate is therefore not a logistical exercise but a legal obligation requiring structured assessment and ongoing oversight.

9.2 Statutory framework

The duties to secure accommodation arise at different stages of the homelessness process and vary according to the nature of the local authority's findings. In practice, the expression "section 188 accommodation" is often used loosely to describe several related but legally distinct situations. As a matter of law, however, section 188 encompasses broadly (i) a mandatory duty to accommodate pending inquiries, and (ii) a discretionary power to accommodate pending review, while accommodation pending appeal arises under a separate statutory provision.

First, section 188(1) of the Housing Act 1996 imposes a mandatory interim accommodation duty pending inquiries. In the event a local authority has reason to believe that an applicant *may be* homeless, eligible for assistance, and in priority need, it must secure suitable accommodation pending completion of its inquiries under section 184. It arises on a deliberately low threshold and is triggered by the possibility that the statutory criteria are met, not by their confirmation. The duty continues until the local authority has completed its inquiries and notified the applicant of a lawful decision under section 184. Accommodation under section 188(1) is therefore obligatory. It is not a matter of discretion and cannot be refused by reference to resource constraints, internal policy, or administrative inconvenience. In fact, where doubt exists as to eligibility, priority need, or homelessness, that doubt ought to be resolved in favour of accommodation until the inquiry process has been lawfully concluded.

Secondly, section 188(3) confers a separate discretionary power to secure accommodation pending a review under section 202. Where an applicant has requested a statutory review of a homelessness decision, the local authority may accommodate the applicant pending the outcome of that review. Unlike accommodation pending inquiries, this is not a duty. However, such discretion should be exercised lawfully, rationally, and on an individual basis. Local authorities should not apply blanket policies or treat refusal as automatic, particularly where the absence of accommodation would undermine the effectiveness of the review process or leave the applicant to immediate homelessness.

Thirdly, accommodation pending appeal arises under section 204(4) rather than section 188. Where an applicant has appealed to the County Court under section 204, the local authority has a discretionary power to secure accommodation pending determination of that appeal. The exercise of this discretion is subject to close scrutiny. Local authorities need to consider the apparent merits of the appeal, the applicant's personal circumstances, any new or changed factors, and whether refusal would cause substantial prejudice to the applicant's ability to pursue their appeal. A refusal to accommodate pending appeal may be challenged by way of the statutory route provided by section 204A. The test for accommodation pending review and appeal will be explained in more detail in Chapter 10.

Section 190 applies where an applicant is found to be intentionally homeless but in priority need. In those circumstances, the local authority should secure accommodation for such period as it considers will give the applicant a reasonable opportunity to obtain alternative accommodation. This is a time-limited duty, but it is nonetheless enforceable and ought to be exercised reasonably and with proper regard to the applicant's circumstances.

Section 193 contains the main housing duty. When an applicant is homeless, eligible, in priority need, and not intentionally homeless, the local authority must secure suitable accommodation until the duty is brought to an end in one of the ways prescribed by the Act, including acceptance of a suitable offer or lawful refusal.

In practice, confusion between the different forms of section 188 accommodation is a frequent source of unlawful decision-making. Local authorities sometimes treat accommodation pending inquiries as discretionary, or apply the more restrictive review or appeal criteria at too early a stage. Equally, discretionary powers pending review or appeal are sometimes exercised as though refusal were the default position. As such, careful identification of the statutory stage reached, and of whether accommodation is owed as a duty or considered as a discretion, is therefore essential.

9.3 The concept of suitability, applicable standards and enforcement

Suitability is a central requirement which governs all accommodation secured under homelessness duties. It is a question of mixed fact and judgment, and requires an assessment of the applicant's individual circumstances against the legal standards derived from statute, case law, and guidance.

That being said, accommodation is suitable only if it offers a reasonable basis for occupation in light of the applicant's needs. The relevant considerations that local authorities have to bear in mind include the size and layout of the accommodation, the physical condition of the property, its location, affordability, and its capacity to accommodate any health or mobility requirements within the household.

Further, overcrowding, unsafe conditions, or accommodation lacking basic facilities will rarely satisfy the suitability requirement. Location is also significant; accommodation that disrupts access to employment, education, medical treatment, or established support networks may be unsuitable, particularly for families with children or applicants with ongoing health needs.

The Homelessness (Suitability of Accommodation) (England) Order 2012 sets out specific statutory standards for suitability. Of particular practical importance is the requirement that bed and breakfast accommodation should not be used for households that include a pregnant woman or dependent children for more than six weeks. Where such accommodation is used beyond that period, the local authority will be in breach of its statutory obligations and the accommodation will not be suitable as a matter of law. Local authorities should be alert to this limit and should take active steps to secure more appropriate accommodation before the six-week period expires. The 2012 Order also requires local authorities to have regard to the location of accommodation in relation to employment, education, and support networks when assessing suitability, reinforcing the general principles discussed above.

Suitability is not a fixed or once-and-for-all assessment. Accommodation that may be lawful and appropriate as a short-term measure can, over time, cease to meet the statutory standard as placements are prolonged or as an applicant's circumstances evolve. Local authorities are therefore under a continuing obligation to keep suitability of said accommodation under active review and to respond where accommodation no longer provides a reasonable or lawful basis for occupation. This duty is ongoing, and compliance is measured not only at the point of placement, but throughout the period for which accommodation is secured.

Enforcing Suitability: Imam v Croydon and Elkundi v Birmingham

Once a local authority has accepted that it owes the main housing duty under section 193(2), or has accepted that accommodation already provided is unsuitable, it is under a continuing statutory obligation to secure suitable accommodation for the applicant. That obligation is not exhausted by the initial placement of accommodation, nor is it suspended by operational difficulty. Suitability ought to be assessed by reference to the applicant's individual circumstances and kept under review for so long as the duty subsists, as explained earlier in Chapter 2.

The legal consequences of prolonged reliance on unsuitable accommodation were clarified by the Supreme Court in *R (Imam) v Croydon LBC* [2023] UKSC 45. The case concerned a failure to provide suitable accommodation to a wheelchair user over an extended period, despite the local authority having accepted that the main housing duty was owed and that the accommodation in question was unsuitable. Croydon resisted a mandatory order on the basis of general assertions about lack of housing stock and financial constraint.

The Supreme Court rejected that approach. Reaffirming long-established principle, the Court held that where Parliament has imposed a clear statutory duty to provide a specific benefit, the duty is assumed to be backed by the resources necessary to fulfil it. A local authority cannot defer compliance by relying on broad statements about scarcity or cost. If a local authority contends that compliance is impossible, it should demonstrate that position with clear, specific, and cogent evidence.

Importantly, the Supreme Court identified a number of factors relevant to the court's discretion when determining the appropriate remedy for breach of section 193(2). These include, first, whether the local authority has access to contingency or flexible funding which could reasonably be deployed to meet the duty, and, if so, why that has not occurred. Secondly, the court may consider whether the local authority was on notice of the unsuitability at an earlier stage and failed to take timely steps to address it. Delay in responding to a known breach may weigh in favour of a mandatory order. Thirdly, the court will assess the impact of the continued breach on the applicant, including the seriousness of the harm caused by the unsuitable accommodation. Fourthly, the absence of any evidence that the local authority is actively progressing towards compliance may support the need for coercive relief. Fifthly, the court must consider fairness to others owed similar duties, ensuring that the applicant is not given improper priority over equally entitled households, while recognising the distinction between duties under Part VII and discretionary allocations under Part VI.

In reaching these conclusions, the Supreme Court emphasised that section 193(2) imposes an immediate and non-deferrable duty to *secure* suitable accommodation. While some short period may be required to determine how best to achieve compliance, the obligation is directed towards an outcome, and that outcome ought to be achieved within a reasonable time. Prolonged reliance on accommodation known to be unsuitable is incompatible with the statutory scheme.

Related guidance on the temporal dimension of the duty was provided by the Court of Appeal in *Elkundi v Birmingham City Council* [2022] EWCA Civ 601. In *Elkundi*, the Court established that once a local authority accepts that the main housing duty is owed, it should ensure that suitable accommodation is actually available to the applicant. By having administrative delay, pending further assessment or decision-making, does not justify leaving an applicant without suitable accommodation. Although *Elkundi* was concerned with the point at which accommodation must be secured, it reinforces the broader principle that the section 193(2) duty should be directed to practical action, and not merely to a process.

Taken together, *Imam* and *Elkundi* establish that suitability under section 193(2) is a concrete legal obligation. Resource pressures, housing shortages, or internal prioritisation cannot, without detailed and specific evidence, justify prolonged non-compliance. Nor may a local authority treat accommodation accepted as unsuitable as an interim holding position while awaiting more favourable conditions.

In practice, these principles require local authorities to demonstrate active and documented efforts to secure suitable accommodation once unsuitability is identified. This includes exploring the use of alternative temporary accommodation, the private rented sector, or adapted properties, and considering whether stock earmarked for Part VI allocation can lawfully be deployed to meet Part VII duties. As such, records should show what steps have been taken, what options have been considered, and why particular routes have not been pursued. Conversely, a local authority's failure to evidence the aforementioned steps is likely to be decisive should the matter come before a court. That said, where delay continues in the absence of a clear explanation or evidence of material efforts, the local authority's ongoing non-compliance may be challenged by way of judicial review. In such cases, the court may be asked to grant declaratory relief or, where appropriate, a mandatory order requiring the local authority to fulfil its duty under section 193(2), as considered further in Chapter 11.

9.4 Out-of-area placements

Section 208(1) of the Housing Act 1996 requires local authorities, so far as reasonably practicable, to secure accommodation within their own district. Although this provision does not expressly mandate placement as close as possible to an applicant's former home, it is settled that the duty requires local authorities, where in-borough accommodation is not reasonably practicable, to seek accommodation as near as possible to the applicant's previous area of residence. This approach recognises that housing decisions have practical consequences for employment, education, medical treatment, and established family and community ties.

In applying section 208(1), local authorities are expected to adopt what has become known as the *concentric-circle approach*. This requires decision-makers to consider accommodation first within the local authority's district, then in neighbouring areas, and only thereafter in more distant locations. The approach is not formulaic, but it imposes a structured obligation to minimise displacement and to ensure that out-of-area placements are driven by necessity rather than administrative convenience.

Out-of-area placements are lawful only where accommodation closer to home is not reasonably practicable at the relevant time. Where such placements are made, the local authority should be able to demonstrate that it has carried out a genuine and reasonable search in accordance with the concentric-circle approach and should record the nature and outcome of that search. Assertions that no closer accommodation was available need to be supported by evidence, not merely stated in final terms.The concentric-circle obligation requires evidence. In *Zaman v Waltham Forest LBC* [2023] EWCA Civ 322, the Court of Appeal established that a local authority must show, by reference to its records, that it actually followed the concentric circle approach rather than simply stating that no closer accommodation was available. Where a local authority has a policy on accommodation acquisition and placement, the question is whether that policy was applied to the individual case. A review decision letter that states the property was the nearest available, without any evidence that the local authority prioritised closer properties or any record of the searches carried out, will not satisfy the obligation. The duty applies to all forms of accommodation the local authority might secure, including private rented sector offers.

Further guidance on the approach to out-of-area placements can be taken from *Nzolameso v Westminster City Council* [2015] UKSC 22. The Supreme Court clarified the nature of the duty imposed by section 208(1). Lady Hale explained that, once accommodation within the local authority's district cannot be secured, the local authority should ordinarily seek to place the household as close as "reasonably practicable" to the area in which it had previously been living. The location of accommodation forms part of its suitability, and the impact of relocation on matters such as children's education, family life, and access to established support must be taken into account. The statutory duty also operates alongside the obligation under section 11 of the Children Act 2004 to have regard to the welfare of children, both in the formulation of policy and in its application to individual cases. A decision to place a household at a distance outside the borough cannot be justified by a general reference to housing shortage alone, and the local authority must be able to explain why accommodation closer to the applicant's area was not reasonably practicable.

It should be noted, this obligation does not end with the initial placement. Where accommodation is accepted out of area, the local authority should reconsider proximity at the date of any subsequent review. The concentric-circle approach therefore applies both at the point of offer and at the point of a review, and requires fresh consideration of whether accommodation nearer to the applicant's original area has since become reasonably practicable.

Importantly, section 208(1) applies to *all* accommodation secured under the homelessness scheme, regardless of the stage of the duty or the tenure of the accommodation. Local authorities should therefore consider not only temporary accommodation but also the availability of private rented sector accommodation and social housing options when assessing proximity. The statutory duty is concerned with the outcome, and accommodation earmarked for other housing functions may, where lawful and appropriate, will need to be considered for the purposes of discharging homelessness duties.

In practice, compliance with section 208(1) requires more than a general awareness of housing pressures. It requires proper searches, recorded reasoning, and a demonstrable effort to place households as close as reasonably practicable to their established area. However, where this structured approach is not followed, decisions on placement are vulnerable to challenge on review or appeal for failure to comply with the statutory scheme.

9.5 Affordability, health, and family considerations

Affordability is a core component of the statutory requirement of suitability and should be addressed as a distinct and substantive issue. Accommodation will not be suitable if, having regard to the applicant's income and resources, it cannot reasonably be afforded after essential living costs are met. Local authorities are therefore required to undertake a reasoned and evidence-based assessment of affordability, taking into account earnings, benefits, rent levels, service charges, and unavoidable household expenditure. This assessment ought to be realistic and grounded in the applicant's actual financial position, rather than based on assumed or notional figures.

Health considerations are equally integral to the suitability analysis. As such where an applicant or member of the household has physical or mental health needs, the local authority should consider whether the accommodation supports stability and access to treatment, including proximity to medical services and continuity of care. This assessment builds on the principles discussed earlier in relation to vulnerability and health-related factors in Chapters 4 and 5, and requires local authorities to give due consideration to medical evidence in a appropriate way, rather than treating health as a peripheral consideration.

For households with children, suitability also requires careful consideration of the impact of accommodation on education and welfare. Disruption to schooling, travel distance, and access to established support networks are all relevant factors, particularly where placements are prolonged or made out of area. Whilst an applicant's inconvenience alone may not render accommodation unsuitable, cumulative disruption may do so where the overall effect on the household is significant.

Local authorities should be able to demonstrate, through clear and contemporaneous records, that affordability, health, and family considerations have been actively assessed and weighed as part of the decision-making process. Unsupported conclusions, generic reasoning, or formulaic references to "having considered all relevant factors" are unlikely to withstand challenge on review or appeal. Suitability requires an evaluative judgment, and the reasoning leading to that judgment should be transparent and intelligible.

In practice, affordability forms a key part of the suitability assessment. Accommodation will not be suitable if the applicant cannot reasonably afford it after meeting essential living costs. Local authorities should therefore undertake a reasoned assessment of income, benefits, rent, and unavoidable expenditure.

Likewise, health considerations are equally important. Applicants with physical or mental health conditions should be taken into account in a manner that supports stability and access to treatment. For families, the impact of accommodation on children's education and welfare should be carefully assessed.

Local authorities should be able to demonstrate through their records that these factors have been properly considered and weighed. Conversely, a local authority's unsupported conclusions or generic reasoning are unlikely to withstand later challenge on review or judicial challenge.

9.6 Duration, termination, and lawful discharge of duty

Temporary accommodation continues for so long as the relevant statutory duty remains in force. It does not ordinarily come to an end by effluxion of time, administrative convenience, or informal decision-making. A local authority's obligation to accommodate continues until the duty is lawfully discharged in one of the limited ways prescribed by statute.

The main housing duty under section 193 of the Housing Act 1996 may be brought to an end only through the mechanisms set out in the Act. These include acceptance of suitable accommodation, refusal of a suitable offer following proper notification and warning, loss of eligibility, or another expressly defined statutory event. Outside those circumstances, the duty is ongoing and suitable accommodation must continue to be secured.

Termination of accommodation should always be carried out lawfully and in accordance with the requirements of procedural fairness. Applicants must be given clear written notice explaining the basis on which the local authority considers the duty to have ended, together with reasons and information about any right to request a review. An eviction or withdrawal of accommodation without proper notice, or on the basis of an uncommunicated decision, may constitute a serious breach of a statutory duty and may give rise to urgent legal remedies.

Local authorities are also required to keep under review the length of time applicants spend in temporary accommodation. As time passes, the local authority's obligations are likely to become more demanding, particularly where accommodation was originally intended to operate as a short-term measure. Any reliance on private rented sector offers to discharge a local authority's duty should be supported by a careful assessment that the accommodation is genuinely suitable, affordable, and capable of being sustained over time.

Bearing that in mind, decisions to terminate accommodation, including findings that a homelessness duty has been "lawfully" discharged per se, are subject to review under section 202 and may, where appropriate, be challenged by appeal or by judicial review, as examined in Chapters 10 and 11.

In practice, unlawful termination of those duties most commonly arises when accommodation is withdrawn on the mistaken assumption that a duty has expired, when refusal of an offer is treated as ending the duty without proper warning or consideration of suitability, or when prolonged delay in securing settled accommodation results in informal pressure on applicants to leave. These risks can be avoided through regular case review, clear audit trails, and strict adherence to the statutory framework. For advisers, close examination of termination decisions frequently reveals procedural defects capable of correction through review or, in urgent cases, judicial intervention.

9.7 Conclusion

Temporary accommodation is a vital mechanism through which the statutory homelessness scheme operates in practice. It is the means by which local authorities perform their statutory obligations under Part VII, not a discretionary welfare provision. What matters is not just whether accommodation exists, but whether it meets the legal standards the statute requires.

Throughout this chapter, the recurring theme has been that temporary accommodation is regulated by law at every stage. A local authority's decisions about placement, duration, affordability, and termination are all matters capable of review and, where necessary, legal challenge. The statutory framework does not permit accommodation to be treated as provisional in a legal sense, even if it is temporary in fact. Once secured under a homelessness duty, accommodation must meet the statutory standard and should continue to do so for as long as the duty remains in force.

For local authorities, lawful administration of temporary accommodation requires structured assessment, careful record-keeping, and regular review. It is an important point to note that resource pressures and operational difficulty do not displace statutory obligations, nor do they justify delay or inaction where accommodation is unsuitable. For applicants and advisers, a clear understanding of the legal framework governing temporary accommodation provides the means by which unlawful practice can be identified and corrected through review, appeal, or judicial oversight, as examined in later chapters.

This chapter illustrates a key principle of homelessness law: that lawful outcomes depend as much on process as on substance. Temporary accommodation fulfils its intended function only where it is secured, maintained, and brought to an end in accordance with the statutory scheme.

CHAPTER TEN

REVIEWS AND APPEALS

10.1 Purpose and structure of the review and appeal system

The review and appeal mechanisms under Part VII of the Housing Act 1996 are the principal safeguards of accountability within homelessness law. They are vital to ensuring that decisions taken by local authorities are open to internal reconsideration and external judicial oversight, and that errors of fact, reasoning, or law can be identified and corrected without immediate recourse to judicial review. In this way, they give practical effect to the public law principles of fairness, transparency, and legality that underpin the statutory scheme.

The review process reflects the reality that homelessness decisions are often taken under significant time pressure, frequently on incomplete or developing information, and sometimes by relatively junior officers. The statutory right to review provides a structured and accessible means of redress, allowing adverse findings to be challenged and errors corrected internally. Appeals to the County Court thereafter provide the necessary judicial supervision to ensure that the law is applied consistently and correctly across local authorities.

The review and appeal framework operates as a core mechanism of accountability within homelessness law. It is not an optional procedural layer, but an essential part of the statutory framework through which lawful decision-making is maintained.

10.2 The right to review (section 202 Housing Act 1996)

Section 202 of the Housing Act 1996 provides applicants a statutory right to request a review of most decisions made under Part VII. It is important to note that such reviews include, amongst others, decisions usually concerning:

- eligibility for assistance;
- whether the applicant is homeless or threatened with homelessness;
- priority need;
- intentional homelessness;
- local connection;
- whether the steps agreed in the Personalised Housing Plan were reasonable under the prevention duty under section 195 or the relief duty under section 189B, including whether those steps were reasonable;
- discharge of relief, prevention or main housing duty and
- the suitability of accommodation offered or provided, including accommodation relied upon to discharge a s193 duty.

In these cases, a request for review must normally be made within 21 days of notification of the local authority's decision, although local authorities retain a discretion to accept late requests where there is a good reason for the delay. The right applies across the full range of homelessness duties, including decisions taken at the interim, prevention, relief, and main duty stages, as well as decisions concerning the suitability of accommodation and final offers.

The review must be carried out by an officer who was not involved in the original decision and who is sufficiently senior to exercise independent judgment. As can be seen, the reviewing officer should acknowledge receipt of the request, explain the review procedure, and allow the applicant a reasonable opportunity to submit further representations or evidence. Applicants may make written submissions and, where appropriate, attend an interview or request an oral meeting. The Allocation of Housing and Homelessness (Review Procedures) Regulations 1999 govern the review procedure in detail, including the circumstances in which an applicant is entitled to request an oral hearing before the review decision is made. Local authorities should be aware of this right and ensure that applicants are informed of it at the outset of the review process.

An applicant may also request a review of the suitability of accommodation under section 202(1)(f) at any time while a duty is being discharged, and not only at the point of an offer. This is a frequently misunderstood point in practice. A local authority that has accepted a main housing duty and is providing temporary accommodation remains subject to a continuing obligation to secure suitable accommodation, and an applicant may request a review of suitability at any point while that duty subsists. Local authorities should not treat the suitability review right as arising only at the point of a final offer.

The right to review is not discretionary. It is a statutory safeguard intended to ensure that decisions affecting access to accommodation and housing stability can be reconsidered lawfully and transparently.

10.3 Conducting the review – procedure and fairness

A review under section 202 is a substantive reconsideration of the homelessness decision. It is not an exercise in checking whether the original conclusion was defensible at the time it was reached. The reviewing officer should instead reassess the decision on the basis of the facts and law as they stand at the date of the review. In addition, the reviewing officer may take into account facts arising after the original decision was made, and any new material provided by the applicant should be considered as part of the review regardless of when it came into existence.

The essential features of a lawful review are as follows:

- **Fresh consideration**

  The reviewing officer ought to approach the matter with an open mind. Findings or assumptions from the original decision should not be treated as determinative and must not be carried forward without independent evaluation.

- **Consideration of all relevant evidence**

  All material relevant to the statutory questions ought to be considered, including any new evidence provided by the applicant after the original decision. This may include updated medical material, housing information, or evidence bearing on suitability and the five tests explained earlier in this book.

- **Application of the correct legal tests**

  Each statutory issue arising under Part VII should be addressed methodically. The reviewing officer should identify the relevant legal test, apply it to the facts found, and avoid conflating distinct questions such as homelessness, priority need, and intentionality.

- **Procedural fairness and disclosure**

  If the review relies on information that is new or adverse and has not previously been disclosed to the applicant, fairness requires that the substance of that material is put to the applicant before the decision is finalised. The applicant needs to be given a reasonable opportunity to respond. Reliance by a local authority on undisclosed adverse material is likely to render the review decision unlawful.

- **Reasoned decision-making**

  The review decision must explain how the outcome has been reached. It should identify the issues considered, summarise the evidence relied upon, make findings of fact, and show how those findings satisfy the statutory framework. Simply repeating or endorsing the wording of the original decision, without fresh analysis, will not meet the statutory requirement.

A properly conducted review acts as a corrective function within the homelessness scheme. It ensures that errors can be identified and rectified internally, and that such decisions are reached through lawful, transparent, and accountable reasoning.

10.4 Appeals to the County Court

An applicant who remains dissatisfied following a homelessness decision may appeal to the County Court under section 204 of the Housing Act 1996. The Act provides different routes of appeal depending on the procedural history of the decision under challenge.

Under section 204(1)(a), an applicant may appeal against a decision made on review under section 202. This is the usual route of appeal and applies where the local authority has completed the internal review process and notified the applicant of the outcome. The appeal must normally be brought within 21 days of notification of the review decision, although the Court has discretion to extend time where it considers it just to do so.

Section 204(1)(b) provides a separate route of appeal where the local authority has failed to notify the applicant of the outcome of a review within the period by which notification should have been given. In such circumstances, the applicant is not required to wait indefinitely and may instead appeal to the County Court on the basis of the authority's failure to notify by the agreed time.

Section 204A performs a distinct and narrower function. It provides a right of appeal to the County Court where an applicant who has brought, or intends to bring, an appeal under section 204 challenges the local authority's refusal to exercise its discretion under section 204(4) to secure accommodation pending determination of the section 204 appeal.

All appeals under sections 204 and 204A lie only on a point of law. The County Court does not conduct a rehearing or substitute its own findings of fact. Instead, it considers whether the local authority misdirected itself in law, failed to make adequate inquiries, took account of irrelevant considerations, failed to consider relevant matters, or reached a conclusion that was irrational in public law terms. In the event where such an appeal succeeds, the Court may quash the decision, vary it, or remit the matter to the local authority for reconsideration.

Issues relating to the arrangement of accommodation pending a section 204 appeal, including the exercise of the discretion under section 204(4) and challenges under section 204A, are addressed separately in Chapter 10.5 below.

10.5 Accommodation pending review or appeal

The arrangement of accommodation pending the outcome of a review or appeal arises at two distinct stages of the statutory process and is governed by different legal principles.

The question of whether accommodation should continue while a homelessness decision is being challenged sits at a sensitive intersection between procedure and substance. It arises after an adverse decision has been made, but before that decision has been finally resolved. Parliament has addressed this period expressly, recognising that the effectiveness of review and appeal rights may be undermined if an applicant is left without accommodation while those processes are ongoing. The statutory framework therefore provides for accommodation pending review and pending appeal, albeit on different terms and subject to different controls.

During the period when a review is pending under section 202 of the Housing Act 1996, the source of the local authority's power to accommodate is section 188(3). Unlike the interim accommodation duty under section 188(1), this is a discretionary power rather than an absolute obligation. That distinction is important, but it does not place the decision beyond legal scrutiny. The discretion ought to be exercised lawfully, rationally, and with regard to the purpose of the statutory scheme. A local authority should therefore consider the request on its merits and should not adopt a blanket policy of refusal or treat accommodation as exceptional.

The practical context here matters. A refusal to accommodate pending review or appeal may leave an applicant street homeless, disrupt access to medical treatment, or even sometimes render the review/appeal process itself ineffective. These consequences are relevant considerations and should be carefully considered and weighed. A failure to consider them, or an automatic refusal without individual assessment, is likely to be unlawful. As such, where a local authority fails to consider, or unlawfully refuses, the act of providing accommodation pending a review under section 202, the appropriate route of challenge will ordinarily be by way of judicial review, a matter addressed in Chapter 11.

A different statutory provision governs accommodation pending appeal to the County Court. In the event where an applicant has brought, or intends to bring, an appeal under section 204, section 204(4) confers a discretion on the local authority to secure accommodation pending determination of that appeal. Although discretionary, this power is tightly constrained by public law principles and by the guidance provided in the case law.

The leading authority remains *R v Camden LBC, ex parte Mohammed* [1997] 30 HLR 315. This case establishes that the exercise of the discretion must involve a structured assessment rather than a cursory or formulaic response. The test includes the apparent merits of the review or appeal, the applicant's personal circumstances and household composition and any material change in circumstances since the decision in question, the period for which accommodation would be needed, and any other material considerations relevant to the individual case.

One consideration carries particular weight in practice: whether refusal to accommodate pending review or appeal would cause substantial prejudice to the applicant. This requires a realistic assessment of consequences. An applicant who would be rendered roofless, prevented from accessing healthcare, or placed at a serious disadvantage in pursuing their review or appeal is likely to suffer substantial prejudice. The more acute the consequences, the stronger the justification required for refusal.

Decisions taken under section 188(3) or section 204(4) must be reasoned and recorded in writing. The applicant is entitled to understand why accommodation has been refused and how the local authority has approached the relevant factors. That said, where a local authority refuses to exercise the discretion under section 204(4), the statutory route of challenge is an appeal to the County Court under section 204A. That mechanism provides focused judicial oversight of a decision which, albeit discretionary, may have immediate and serious consequences for the applicant.

10.6 Common errors and good practice

Experience drawn from both practice and the case law reveals a familiar pattern of difficulty in the operation of homelessness reviews and appeals. Such errors often arise not from the absence of statutory powers, but from the manner in which those powers are exercised. Common shortcomings include failure to grapple with fresh or updated evidence, reliance on formulaic or inadequate reasoning, the uncritical repetition of earlier decision letters, and misunderstanding or misapplication of the statutory tests.

It is important to note that proper administration of those duties requires more than formal compliance with section 202. Reviews ought to be conducted by officers who are both independent of the original decision and equipped with the necessary legal and procedural understanding. A lawful review is intended to be carried out in a structured and methodical way, identifying the issues to be determined, assessing the evidence with care, applying the correct legal framework, and explaining how the conclusion has been reached. Bearing this in mind, decisions that demonstrate this reasoning on their face are more likely to be legally correct and to withstand scrutiny by applicants. That being said, accurate record-keeping and clear communication are indispensable to that process, underpinning both procedural fairness and the defensibility of outcomes.

As set out in this chapter, the review and appeal framework occupies a vital position within Part VII of the Housing Act 1996. It is the primary means by which defective decisions can be corrected without immediate recourse to judicial action, while also providing the route through which appellate courts shape and clarify the law. When these mechanisms are used properly, they reinforce consistency, accountability, and legality across the statutory scheme, ensuring that homelessness decision-making operates in the manner Parliament intended.

CHAPTER ELEVEN

JUDICIAL REVIEW

Judicial review is the mechanism through which the courts hold local authorities to account where statutory processes have failed or been bypassed. It ensures that local authorities stay within the limits of their statutory powers and act in accordance with public law standards. Within the homelessness context, judicial review plays an important role because decisions about housing often determine whether an individual or family has access to accommodation, health, and stability. Judicial review is not a substitute for the statutory review and appeal processes under Part VII of the Housing Act 1996; it is designed to ensure that decision-makers act within the scope of their legal powers and adhere to proper standards of decision-making. In homelessness law, judicial review often arises where statutory processes are unavailable, have been bypassed, or where unlawful delay or procedural defect has occurred. In emergency situations — such as failure to accept a homelessness application or to provide interim accommodation — judicial review may be the only effective remedy available in time-critical circumstances.

11.1 When Judicial Review Is Appropriate

Judicial review is appropriate where no other adequate remedy exists, or where statutory processes have been undermined by procedural error, inaction, or delay. In the context of homelessness law, this most commonly arises where the statutory machinery has failed at an early stage, or where the protections built into the scheme have not been acted upon at all. Typical examples include a local authority's refusal to accept a homelessness application under section 183 of the Housing Act 1996 despite having reason to believe that the applicant may be homeless or threatened with homelessness, or the local authority otherwise acting outside its statutory powers or in breach of the principles of procedural fairness and public law.

Given homelessness decisions frequently determine an applicant's immediate living conditions, the courts are prepared to grant urgent relief—sometimes within a very short timeframe—to prevent irreparable harm. Yet all too often, this reflects the reality that delay or procedural obstruction can render substantive statutory rights ineffective. Judicial review in this field should therefore be understood as a protective jurisdiction, designed to secure lawful administration and ensure compliance with Parliament's scheme, rather than as a punitive response to administrative failure.

As explained in Chapter 8, the statutory framework can be deliberately triggered at a low threshold. The duty to accept and investigate a homeless application arises as soon as the local authority has reason to believe that the applicant may be homeless or threatened with homelessness. A failure to honour that obligation will, in many cases, leave judicial review as the applicant's only recourse.

In practice, judicial review most often arises in homelessness cases where delay or refusal has left an applicant without effective access to the statutory scheme. A local authority's failures to accept an application, to provide interim accommodation where the threshold is met, or to make timely decisions following clear requests for assistance frequently require urgent intervention. In such cases, the availability of swift judicial oversight serves as a critical safeguard, ensuring that statutory duties are not eroded by administrative inertia and that applicants are not left without remedy at the very point when the legal framework is intended to offer protection.

11.2 Grounds of Challenge: Illegality, Irrationality, and Procedural Unfairness

The established grounds for judicial review form the foundation of administrative law and apply with full force in homelessness cases. They provide the framework through which the courts assess whether a local authority has exercised its statutory functions lawfully. In homelessness practice, these grounds regularly come into issue and have direct, practical consequences for decision-making. These grounds include:

Illegality arises where a local authority acts outside the scope of its statutory powers, misdirects itself as to the applicable legal test, or fails to take into account a consideration which the statute requires it to address. In homelessness practice, this commonly includes applying the wrong test for homelessness, priority need, or intentionality, or failing to have regard to relevant rules of the Housing Act 1996, associated regulations, or statutory guidance.

Irrationality, often described as Wednesbury unreasonableness, concerns the substance of the decision reached. A decision will be unlawful if it is so unreasonable that no reasonable local authority, properly directing itself in law, could have reached it. In the homelessness context, this may include conclusions that are plainly inconsistent or untenable with the evidence, disregard material facts, or rest on assumptions that are not supported by the inquiry undertaken.

Procedural unfairness focuses on the manner in which the decision was reached. Even a decision that is substantively correct may be unlawful if the process was unfair. Procedural unfairness may arise where an applicant is not informed of adverse material, is denied a proper opportunity to respond, or where decisions are taken without adequate inquiry. Such fairness requires that applicants understand the substance of the case against them and are given a real opportunity to participate in the decision-making process.

These grounds are not merely technical constructs. In fact, they provide concrete effect to the rule of law by ensuring that homelessness decisions are made within legal limits, based on rational evaluation, and through processes that respect basic standards of fairness.

Accordingly, successful challenges often involve an overlap between these grounds. A failure to make adequate inquiries may amount simultaneously to illegality and procedural unfairness; a decision that ignores compelling evidence may engage more than one ground of challenge. For advisers, careful analysis of how the local authority approached the decision—what it considered, what it ignored, and how it reasoned—is frequently decisive in identifying a viable ground of challenge

Common Grounds in Urgent Homelessness Judicial Reviews

Urgent homelessness judicial reviews most frequently arise from failures at the entry points of the statutory scheme or from unlawful withdrawal of accommodation. The following grounds recur in practice:

- **Failure to accept an application**

  A refusal to take a homelessness application despite there being reason to believe the applicant may be homeless or threatened with homelessness, contrary to sections 183–184 of the Housing Act 1996.

- **Unlawful refusal or withdrawal of interim accommodation**

  Failure to provide accommodation under section 188 where the low threshold is met, or withdrawal of accommodation before a lawful decision is notified.

- **Defective or delayed decision-making**

  Excessive delay in completing inquiries or making a section 184 decision, rendering statutory rights ineffective in practice.

- **Misapplication of statutory tests**

  Use of incorrect legal standards for homelessness, priority need, intentionality, or suitability, including failure to apply binding case law.

In urgent cases, the court's focus is typically on restoring lawful process rather than determining substantive entitlement. Interim relief is often sought to reinstate accommodation or compel a local authority's compliance with statutory duties pending lawful determination.

11.3 Legitimate Expectation and Proportionality

In addition to the classic grounds of illegality, irrationality, and procedural unfairness, two further public law doctrines frequently arise in judicial review of homelessness decisions: legitimate expectation and proportionality. Both operate as controls on how statutory powers are exercised, rather than as freestanding sources of substantive entitlement.

Legitimate expectation arises where a local authority, through an express promise, a settled practice, or a published policy, has led an applicant reasonably to expect that it will act in a particular way. In the homelessness context, this most commonly concerns adherence to published policies on matters such as interim accommodation, suitability assessments, review procedures, or the handling of out-of-area placements. Likewise, when such an expectation has been relied upon, the local authority may not lawfully depart from it without good reason, and ordinarily not without first providing the applicant an opportunity to make representations. A failure to honour a legitimate expectation, or to explain and justify a departure from it, may render a decision unlawful even where the local authority may retain a broad statutory discretion.

Proportionality often arises through the Human Rights Act 1998, particularly where homelessness decisions interfere with rights protected by Article 8 of the European Convention on Human Rights. Whilst Article 8 may not confer a general right to housing, decisions that result in eviction, withdrawal of accommodation, or enforced relocation may constitute an interference insofar as private or family life is concerned. In such cases, the court will consider whether the interference pursues a legitimate aim, whether it is rationally connected to that aim, and whether it goes no further than is necessary to achieve it. The availability of less intrusive alternatives can be a key consideration.

In homelessness cases, proportionality analysis frequently overlaps with questions of suitability, fairness, and reasoned decision-making, particularly where the practical consequence of a decision is street homelessness or serious disruption to family life. Although proportionality does not displace the statutory framework under Part VII of the Housing Act 1996, it informs the manner in which discretionary powers should be exercised and provides an additional lens through which the lawfulness of decisions may be assessed.

Legitimate expectation and proportionality reflect a modern public law approach that emphasises transparency, consistency, and respect for an applicant's fundamental rights. They reinforce the principle that, even where Parliament has conferred discretion on local authorities, that discretion ought to be exercised rationally, fairly, and in a manner that is properly justified by reference to both policy and individual circumstances.

11.4 Pre-Action Protocol and Procedure

Judicial review is governed by a procedural framework designed to promote early resolution and to ensure that public bodies are given a fair opportunity to address alleged unlawfulness before proceedings are issued. In England, an applicant is ordinarily required to comply with the Pre-Action Protocol for Judicial Review before commencing a claim.

The protocol requires the applicant, or their legal representative, to notify the local authority of the proposed challenge and to set out the basis upon which the decision is said to be unlawful. This step serves to crystallise the issues in dispute, to promote focused decision-making, and, in appropriate cases, to enable the local authority to correct errors without recourse to litigation.

A pre-action letter will ordinarily include:

- a clear and thorough summary of the factual background and the decision or omission being challenged;
- the legal grounds upon which the challenge is advanced;
- the remedy sought, such as an action or reinstatement of accommodation, or reconsideration of a decision in accordance with the law; and
- a clear timeframe for response, tailored to the urgency of the situation.

Local authorities are expected to acknowledge and respond substantively within a reasonable period. In homelessness cases, this is often between 14 and 21 days, although significantly shorter timescales may be appropriate where the applicant faces immediate loss of accommodation or other urgent harm.

If the matter is not resolved through the pre-action process, or if urgency makes compliance impracticable, the applicant may issue proceedings in the Administrative Court. Judicial review claims should be brought promptly and, in any event, within three months of the date on which the grounds of challenge first arose, subject to any applicable procedural requirements or statutory time limits.

In practice, effective use of the pre-action protocol frequently resolves homelessness disputes at an early stage. In the event that litigation does follow, compliance with the protocol assists the court in identifying the real issues and may be relevant to the exercise of its discretion on costs.

11.5 Urgent and Interim Relief

Judicial review claims in homelessness cases frequently involve applications for urgent relief, given the potentially serious and immediate consequences of losing accommodation. The court has broad powers to make interim orders, including:

- requiring a local authority to provide or reinstate temporary or interim accommodation pending determination of the claim;
- prohibiting eviction or withdrawal of services; or
- directing the local authority to reconsider a decision or omission immediately.

Interim relief is discretionary and will be granted where there is a serious issue to be tried, where the applicant is likely to suffer irreparable harm without relief, and where the balance of convenience favours interim protection. In urgent claims, witness evidence accompanying such applications may be necessary and should clearly set out the factual background, the decision or omission being challenged, and the consequences of refusing relief.

11.6 Costs and Remedies

When a judicial review claim succeeds, the court may grant remedies including:

- a quashing order, setting aside the unlawful decision;
- a mandatory order, compelling the local authority to act or make a fresh decision;
- a prohibiting order, restraining unlawful action;
- a declaration, clarifying legal rights or obligations; and
- damages, for example where a breach of the Human Rights Act 1998 is established.

In many claims, the general rule is that costs follow the event, although courts retain discretion, particularly where conduct has been unreasonable or where a claim succeeds only in part.

Judicial review is the primary mechanism through which the courts hold local authorities to account within homelessness law. It ensures that local authorities act within the limits of their statutory authority and in accordance with public law principles. For applicants, it offers a critical route to challenge unlawful decisions where statutory remedies are unavailable or ineffective. Likewise, for local authorities, it provides an incentive for lawful and reasoned decision-making.

CHAPTER TWELVE

GOOD PRACTICE AND PRACTICAL GUIDANCE

Homelessness law operates at the point where statutory powers meet day-to-day administrative decision-making. Unlike many areas of public law, decisions taken under Part VII of the Housing Act 1996 have immediate and practical consequences. The acceptance of an application (see Chapter 8), the provision of interim accommodation (see Chapter 9), and the bringing of a duty to an end following review or appeal (see Chapter 10) will often determine an applicant's living arrangements within hours or days.

In the homelessness context, good practice ensures that statutory duties under the Housing Act 1996 and the Homelessness Reduction Act 2017 are exercised consistently, accurately, and in accordance with public law principles. It produces better decisions, and limits the need for review, appeal, or judicial intervention (see Chapters 10 and 11). Importantly, good practice does not require leniency or informality. It requires technical competence, structured reasoning, and adherence to lawful process, even in difficult circumstances or under operational pressure.

This chapter draws together practical guidance that supports lawful homelessness decision-making across the full lifecycle of an application. It should be read alongside the detailed analysis of statutory duties in Chapter 2, the substantive tests of eligibility, homelessness, priority need, intentionality and local connection in Chapters 3 to 7, and the procedural safeguards addressed in Chapters 8 to 11.

12.1 Early Intervention and Prevention

Early intervention is central to the modern statutory homelessness framework. The prevention duty introduced by the Homelessness Reduction Act 2017 reflects Parliament's recognition that homelessness is rarely a sudden event. It is more often the end point of a sequence of identifiable risks and failures, which, if addressed in time, may prevent the loss of accommodation altogether. Part VII therefore places deliberate emphasis on early enquiries, before actual homelessness begins and before more onerous statutory duties arise.

From a legal perspective, prevention is not concerned with the outcome alone, but with a proper and reasoned approach. As explained in Chapter 2, the duty under section 195 requires local authorities to take *reasonable steps* to help an eligible applicant to secure that their accommodation does not cease to be available. However, what constitutes reasonable steps is inherently contextual and depends upon the nature of the risk to the applicant's accommodation, the applicant's circumstances, and the housing options realistically available. The assessment requires an informed understanding of how housing insecurity develops and how particular factors interact with an individual's capacity to sustain their accommodation.

It is important to note that certain indicators recur frequently in practice and can provide a reliable basis for the commencement of enquiries. These often include the accumulation of rent arrears, service of a notice seeking possession, relationship breakdown, the expiry of a fixed-term tenancy, discharge from institutional accommodation, or deterioration in physical or mental health. None of these factors is determinative in itself. Rather, their legal significance lies in the fact that, taken individually or cumulatively, they may give a local authority reason to believe that homelessness is threatened within the statutory timeframe. Once that threshold is met, the prevention duty is activated.

The discharge of the prevention duty commonly requires structured and targeted action on an applicant's circumstances. Reasonable steps may vary, but the statutory scheme assumes active intervention rather than passive signposting. In practice, effective prevention commonly involves:

- the establishment of clear internal referral mechanisms so that housing risk identified by any department of the local authority is promptly escalated;
- ongoing liaison with registered providers and private landlords, including negotiation around arrears, possession proceedings, or tenancy terms;
- targeted use of Discretionary Housing Payments and prevention funding to address shortfalls which would otherwise lead to loss of accommodation; and
- coordination between housing services and welfare, debt, or employment support, where the risk of homelessness arises from financial instability rather than housing supply alone.

Notably, preventative activity ought to be properly recorded and actioned. Clear records demonstrate not only compliance with section 195, but also allow the adequacy of any steps taken to be reviewed under section 202, and provide essential context if the applicant later presents as homeless and issues of intentionality or suitability arise. In this sense, prevention is not a preliminary or optional phase of the homelessness process. Instead, it is a vital part of the legal scheme through which later duties are shaped and, in many cases, avoided.

In practice, disputes concerning the prevention duty most often arise not from the absence of any action, but from disagreement as to whether the steps taken were reasonable in the circumstances. Local authorities that can demonstrate early identification of risk, informed assessments, and a coherent course of action are far better placed to defend their decisions on review or legal challenge. Conversely, generic plans, delay in making enquiries, or reliance on unsupported assumptions about an applicant's ability to resolve matters independently are unlikely to withstand challenge on review.

12.2 Vulnerable Applicants and Reasonable Adjustments

Vulnerability in homelessness administration extends beyond the statutory concept of priority need addressed in Chapter 5. It includes any factor that materially affects an applicant's ability to participate effectively in the process, communicate their circumstances, or protect their own interests. As explained earlier, vulnerability may arise from disability, mental ill-health, trauma, learning difficulty, language barriers, addiction, serious illness, or social isolation.

One thing that should be noted is that local authorities must exercise their homelessness functions in compliance with the Equality Act 2010. This includes the duty to make reasonable adjustments for disabled applicants and the Public Sector Equality Duty under section 149, which applies across all stages of the homelessness process, including inquiries under section 184 (Chapter 8), suitability assessments (Chapter 9), and reviews under section 202 (Chapter 10).

Reasonable adjustments may include:

- providing interpreters or translation services;
- allowing additional time for interviews or representations;
- conducting interviews in accessible or appropriate locations;
- adapting written communication into accessible formats; and
- ensuring officers are trained to recognise and respond to trauma-related presentation.

Similarly, local authorities should record what adjustments were considered and implemented, and why. Failure to properly consider reasonable adjustments may render a decision unlawful and open the local authority to challenge by review or judicial review (see Chapters 10 and 11).

12.3 Record-Keeping and Communication

Throughout this book, and in particular in Chapters 8, 9 and 10, the statutory scheme has been shown to depend not merely on the correctness of outcomes, but on the ability of a local authority to demonstrate how those outcomes were reached. Any local authority's decisions made under Part VII should be capable of reconstruction. This means a conclusion unsupported by a discernible evidential and reasoning trail is prone to challenge, not because it is necessarily wrong, but because it cannot be shown to be right.

In practice, record-keeping performs a number of distinct legal functions. It preserves the factual basis upon which statutory tests have been applied; it enables effective internal review under section 202; and it provides the material against which a court may assess lawfulness on appeal or judicial review. In this sense, records are not ancillary to decision-making; instead they are the medium through which decision-making can be rendered accountable.

In practice, a properly maintained applicant's case file will ordinarily contain contemporaneous notes of key interactions and inquiries. This will include records of interviews and telephone discussions, correspondence with applicants and third parties, internal deliberations relevant to the application of statutory tests, and copies of documents relied upon, such as medical evidence, tenancy documentation, or possession notices. Likewise, entries should be dated, attributed, and sufficiently precise to allow a reviewing officer or court to understand what information was available at the time and how it informed the local authority's reasoning.

What is clear is that deficiencies in record-keeping are a recurrent feature of successful challenges by applicants. Inadequate notes, missing documents, or unexplained conclusions frequently undermine decisions on review under section 202 and can open local authorities to judicial scrutiny. The difficulty is rarely that a local authority lacked a lawful basis for its decision; more often, it is that the basis cannot be demonstrated after the event.

Communication is the counterpart to record-keeping in ensuring procedural fairness. A decision that is fully reasoned internally but inadequately explained to the applicant may remain procedurally flawed. Written notifications should do more than state an outcome. Rather they ought to identify the statutory rule under which the decision has been made, explain how the relevant legal tests have been applied to the facts found, and set out the applicant's rights to review or appeal, as explained in Chapter 10.

It is perhaps then little surprise that effective communication also requires sensitivity to practical barriers in this context. In other words, where applicants face literacy, language, or cognitive difficulties, reasonable steps should be taken to ensure that decisions are properly understood by the applicant, not merely made. Where communication is inadequate, an applicant may be unable to exercise their right of review effectively, rendering the decision procedurally defective.

12.4 Technology, Data and Artificial Intelligence in Homelessness Decision-Making

Homelessness administration may increasingly rely on digital case management systems, shared data platforms, and automated tools. These systems may support consistency, efficiency, and early identification of risk, but they do not alter the statutory framework set out in Part VII of the Housing Act 1996. Legal responsibility for homelessness decisions remains with the local authority and its officers. Unlike traditional case-management software, generative systems are capable of producing fluent narrative outputs that resemble formal decision letters, legal reasoning, and statutory analysis. This capability presents distinct legal risks which go beyond efficiency or record-keeping concerns.

A particular danger lies in the apparent plausibility of AI-generated reasoning. Generative systems can produce outputs that correctly reference statutory provisions, case law, and established legal tests, while simultaneously misapplying those principles to the facts of an individual case. Given the language used may often appear structured and legally literate, errors may not be immediately obvious, either to officers relying on the output or to applicants receiving it. The risk is not limited to clerical error, it may give rise to substantive legal mistakes that are not apparent from the face of the decision.

Bearing this in mind, homelessness decision-making may illustrate this risk in practice. Statutory concepts such as vulnerability, priority need, suitability, and intentionality require evaluative judgment informed by the applicant's individual circumstances. It is important to note that these judgments cannot lawfully be pre-determined, framed, or steered by a system that is indifferent to evidential weight, credibility, or cumulative impact. A system capable of generating mutually inconsistent outcomes from identical factual material draws attention to the point: which may mean that the appearance of legal reasoning does not equate to the exercise of lawful discretion.

The opacity of generative AI systems makes this more difficult. In these circumstances, where prompts, intermediate reasoning, or AI model constraints are not preserved, the local authority may be unable to explain how a particular conclusion was reached. This undermines the fundamental requirement, examined throughout Chapters 8 to 10, that decisions be reasoned and capable of challenge on review or appeal. In that sense, a local authority may not be able to properly defend a decision if it cannot identify the reasoning process by which it was made.

There are also equality implications. Automated or AI-assisted reasoning may fail to identify, or may inadvertently discount, vulnerabilities arising from trauma, mental ill-health, learning difficulty, or domestic abuse. If such failures disproportionately affect protected groups, the local authority may be unable to demonstrate compliance with the Public Sector Equality Duty.

For these reasons, any use of generative AI within homelessness functions should be approached with caution. If used at all, such tools ought to be confined to clearly administrative tasks and should not be permitted to frame, determine, or materially influence statutory findings. Officers ought to remain fully responsible for identifying the relevant legal tests, weighing evidence, and reaching conclusions on vulnerability, priority need, suitability, or discharge of duty. Decision letters should reflect the housing officer's own reasoning, not an automated synthesis.

Local authorities should therefore ensure that:

- automated outputs are treated as advisory rather than determinative;
- all information relied upon is verified against primary sources;
- decision-making processes remain auditable and transparent; and
- data protection obligations under the Data Protection Act 2018 and UK GDPR are met.

In practice, whilst technology can support strategic planning and prevention work, it should not be used to filter out applications or pre-empt statutory inquiries. Rather, local authorities should assume that any homelessness decision materially influenced by unrecorded or unexamined AI output will likely be prone to challenge. Likewise, where a decision cannot be explained without reference to an automated process, or where reasoning appears formulaic or internally inconsistent, advisers should consider whether the decision has in fact been lawfully made at all. The requirement that statutory duties be discharged through rational, transparent, and accountable decision-making applies regardless of the tools employed. Technology may assist decision makers, but it cannot lawfully replace human judgment.

12.5 Concluding Reflections

Good practice and legal compliance are the same thing in homelessness law. Decisions made on proper inquiry, with clear reasoning, are both better administration and better law. The framework examined throughout this book is deliberately structured and procedural. Its effectiveness depends on the consistent application of the statutory tests and legal standards prescribed by Parliament.

Those tests are examined in detail in Chapters 3 to 7, which address eligibility, homelessness, priority need, intentional homelessness, and local connection. Each involves defined legal criteria, informed by statute and case law, which should be applied to the facts of the individual case through careful inquiry and reasoned judgment. The accuracy with which these tests are applied determines whether duties arise, what form they take, and how long they last.

From the local authority's preliminary enquiries of an applicant in Chapter 8, through the assessment and arrangement of accommodation in Chapters 9 and 10, to review, appeal, and judicial oversight in Chapter 11, the statutory scheme requires proper inquiry, accurate record-keeping, and clear reasoning. These are not optional features of good administration. Rather they are the means by which decisions are made lawfully and through which applicants can exercise the rights Parliament has given them.

Although operational pressures are a constant feature of homelessness administration, they do not alter the content of statutory duties or the threshold tests that govern them. Local authorities that adopt a structured and timely approach to reviewing their decisions are better placed to apply the legal tests consistently and to avoid challenge on review or in the courts.

The homelessness system works when officers know the law, apply it carefully, and explain their reasoning. Decisions based on proper inquiries into an applicant's circumstances, correct application of the statutory criteria, and lawful process are more likely to produce outcomes that are right.

MORE BOOKS BY LAW BRIEF PUBLISHING

A selection of our other titles available now:-

‘The Electronic Communications Code: A Practical Guide – Second Edition’ by Kerry Bretherton KC, James Castle, Mark Loveday

‘A Practical Guide to the Independent School Standards – September 2023 Edition’ by Sarah McKimm

'A Practical Guide to Estate Administration and Crypto Assets' by Richard Marshall

‘A Practical Guide to Parental Alienation in Private and Public Law Children Cases’ by Sam King QC & Frankie Shama

‘Contested Heritage – Removing Art from Land and Historic Buildings’ by Richard Harwood QC, Catherine Dobson, David Sawtell

‘The Limits of Separate Legal Personality: When Those Running a Company Can Be Held Personally Liable for Losses Caused to Third Parties Outside of the Company’ by Dr Mike Wilkinson

‘A Practical Guide to Transgender Law’ by Robin Moira White & Nicola Newbegin

‘A Practical Guide to ‘Stranded Spouses’ in Family Law’ by Mani Singh Basi

‘A Practical Guide to Residential Freehold Conveyancing’ by Lorraine Richardson

‘A Practical Guide to Pensions on Divorce for Lawyers’ by Bryan Scant

‘A Practical Guide to Challenging Sham Marriage Allegations in Immigration Law’ by Priya Solanki

‘A Practical Guide to Digital Communications Evidence in Criminal Law’ by Sam Willis

‘A Practical Guide to Legal Rights in Scotland’ by Sarah-Jane Macdonald

‘A Practical Guide to New Build Conveyancing’ by Paul Sams & Rebecca East

‘A Practical Guide to Inherited Wealth on Divorce’ by Hayley Trim

‘A Practical Guide to Practice Direction 12J and Domestic Abuse in Private Law Children Proceedings’ by Rebecca Cross & Malvika Jaganmohan

‘A Practical Guide to Confiscation and Restraint’ by Narita Bahra QC, John Carl Townsend, David Winch

‘A Practical Guide to the Law of Forests in Scotland’ by Philip Buchan

‘A Practical Guide to Health and Medical Cases in Immigration Law’ by Rebecca Chapman & Miranda Butler

‘A Practical Guide to Bad Character Evidence for Criminal Practitioners by Aparna Rao

‘A Practical Guide to Extradition Law post-Brexit’ by Myles Grandison et al

‘A Practical Guide to Hoarding and Mental Health for Housing Lawyers’ by Rachel Coyle

'Stephens on Contractual Indemnities' by Richard Stephens
'A Practical Guide to the EU Succession Regulation' by Richard Frimston
'A Practical Guide to Solicitor and Client Costs – Second Edition' by Robin Dunne
'Constructive Dismissal – Practice Pointers and Principles' by Benjimin Burgher
'A Practical Guide to Religion and Belief Discrimination Claims in the Workplace' by Kashif Ali
'A Practical Guide to the Law of Medical Treatment Decisions' by Ben Troke
'Fundamental Dishonesty and QOCS in Personal Injury Proceedings: Law and Practice' by Jake Rowley
'A Practical Guide to the Law in Relation to School Exclusions' by Charlotte Hadfield & Alice de Coverley
'A Practical Guide to Divorce for the Silver Separators' by Karin Walker
'The Right to be Forgotten – The Law and Practical Issues' by Melissa Stock
'A Practical Guide to Planning Law and Rights of Way in National Parks, the Broads and AONBs' by James Maurici QC, James Neill et al
'A Practical Guide to Election Law' by Tom Tabori
'A Practical Guide to the Law in Relation to Surrogacy' by Andrew Powell
'A Practical Guide to Claims Arising from Fatal Accidents – Second Edition' by James Patience
'A Practical Guide to Asbestos Claims' by Jonathan Owen & Gareth McAloon
'A Practical Guide to Stamp Duty Land Tax in England and Northern Ireland' by Suzanne O'Hara
'A Practical Guide to the Law of Farming Partnerships' by Philip Whitcomb
'A Practical Guide to the Law of Unlawful Eviction and Harassment – Second Edition' by Stephanie Lovegrove
'A Practical Guide to Costs in Personal Injury Claims – Second Edition' by Matthew Hoe
'A Practical Guide to the General Data Protection Regulation (GDPR) – Second Edition' by Keith Markham
'A Practical Guide to Working with Litigants in Person and McKenzie Friends in Family Cases' by Stuart Barlow
'Protecting Unregistered Brands: A Practical Guide to the Law of Passing Off' by Lorna Brazell
'A Practical Guide to Secondary Liability and Joint Enterprise Post-Jogee' by Joanne Cecil & James Mehigan

'A Practical Guide to the Pre-Action RTA Claims Protocol for Personal Injury Lawyers' by Antonia Ford
'A Practical Guide to Neighbour Disputes and the Law' by Alexander Walsh
'A Practical Guide to Coercive Control for Legal Practitioners and Victims' by Rachel Horman
'A Practical Guide to the Law of Driverless Cars – Second Edition'
by Alex Glassbrook, Emma Northey & Scarlett Milligan
'A Practical Guide to TOLATA Claims' by Greg Williams
'A Practical Guide to Elderly Law – Second Edition' by Justin Patten
'A Practical Guide to Responding to Housing Disrepair and Unfitness Claims' by Iain Wightwick
'A Practical Guide to the Law of Bullying and Harassment in the Workplace' by Philip Hyland
'How to Be a Freelance Solicitor: A Practical Guide to the SRA-Regulated Freelance Solicitor Model' by Paul Bennett
'A Practical Guide to Prison Injury Claims' by Malcolm Johnson
'A Practical Guide to Advising Clients at the Police Station' by Colin Stephen McKeown-Beaumont
'A Practical Guide to Antisocial Behaviour Injunctions – Second Edition' by Iain Wightwick
'Practical Mediation: A Guide for Mediators, Advocates, Advisers, Lawyers, and Students in Civil, Commercial, Business, Property, Workplace, and Employment Cases' by Jonathan Dingle with John Sephton
'The Mini-Pupillage Workbook' by David Boyle
'A Practical Guide to Crofting Law' by Brian Inkster
'A Practical Guide to the Law of Domain Names and Cybersquatting' by Andrew Clemson
'A Practical Guide to the Law of Gender Pay Gap Reporting' by Harini Iyengar
'NHS Whistleblowing and the Law' by Joseph England
'Employment Law and the Gig Economy' by Nigel Mackay & Annie Powell
'A Practical Guide to Noise Induced Hearing Loss (NIHL) Claims' by Andrew Mckie, Ian Skeate, Gareth McAloon
'An Introduction to Beauty Negligence Claims – A Practical Guide for the Personal Injury Practitioner' by Greg Almond
'Intercompany Agreements for Transfer Pricing Compliance' by Paul Sutton
'Zen and the Art of Mediation' by Martin Plowman
'A Practical Guide to Adoption for Family Lawyers' by Graham Pegg

'A Practical Guide to Industrial Disease Claims' by Andrew Mckie & Ian Skeate

'A Practical Guide to Conducting a Sheriff Court Proof' by Andrew Stevenson

'A Practical Guide to Vicarious Liability' by Mariel Irvine

'A Practical Guide to Applications for Landlord's Consent and Variation of Leases' by Mark Shelton

'A Practical Guide to Relief from Sanctions Post-Mitchell and Denton' by Peter Causton

'A Practical Guide to Equity Release for Advisors' by Paul Sams

'A Practical Guide to Financial Services Claims' by Chris Hegarty

'A Practical Guide to Financial Ombudsman Service Claims' by Adam Temple & Robert Scrivenor

'A Practical Guide to Running Housing Disrepair and Cavity Wall Claims – Second Edition' by Andrew Mckie & Ian Skeate

'A Practical Guide to Holiday Sickness Claims – Second Edition' by Andrew Mckie & Ian Skeate

'Arguments and Tactics for Personal Injury and Clinical Negligence Claims' by Dorian Williams

'A Practical Guide to Drone Law' by Rufus Ballaster, Andrew Firman, Eleanor Clot

'On Experts: CPR35 for Lawyers and Experts' by David Boyle

'An Introduction to Personal Injury Law' by David Boyle

These books and more are available to order online direct from the publisher at www.lawbriefpublishing.com, where you can also read free sample chapters. For any queries, call us on 0844 587 2383 or email us at mail@lawbriefpublishing.com.

Our books are all generally in stock at www.amazon.co.uk with free next day delivery for Prime members, and at good legal bookshops such as Wildy & Sons.

We are regularly launching new books in our series of practical day-to-day practitioners' guides. Visit our website and join our free newsletter to be kept informed and to receive special offers, free chapters, etc.

You can also follow us on Twitter at www.twitter.com/lawbriefpub.

www.ingramcontent.com/pod-product-compliance
Lightning Source LLC
LaVergne TN
LVHW050303210926
848481LV00014BA/806
* 9 7 8 1 9 1 8 2 4 1 3 5 8 *